© Scripture Union 2005

First published 2005

ISBN 1 84427 189 7

Scripture Union, 207–209 Queensway, Bletchley, Milton Keynes, MK2 2EB, UK
Email: info@scriptureunion.org.uk
Website: www.scriptureunion.org.uk

Scripture Union Australia, Locked Bag 2, Central Coast Business Centre, NSW 2252, Australia
Website: www.scriptureunion.org.au

Scripture Union USA, PO Box 987, Valley Forge, PA 19482, USA
Website: www.scriptureunion.org

Scripture quotations are from the Contemporary English Version © American Bible Society 1991, 1992,
1995. Anglicisations © British and Foreign Bible Society 1997, published in the UK by
HarperCollins*Publishers*. Used by permission.

British Library Cataloguing-in-Publication Data.
A catalogue record of this biook is available from the British Library.

Printed and bound in Malta by Progress Print.

Cover design: Paul Airy
Internal design: Alex Taylor
Compiler: Christine Wright
Artists: Pauline Adams, Alex Ayliffe, Clive Edwards and Andy Robb

Scripture Union is an international charity working with churches in more than 130 countries,
providing resources to bring the good news of Jesus Christ to children, young people and families
and to encourage them to develop spiritually through the Bible and prayer.

As well as our network of volunteers, staff and associates who run holidays, church-based events and
school Christian groups, we produce a wide range of publications and support those who use our
resources through training programmes.

Contents

Easter is the high point of the Christian year! It has been celebrated by the Christian church from its very beginning. Although Christmas is more widely observed in today's society, it is Easter that holds the true meaning of the Christian faith.

So let's celebrate it together! Easter Cracked is packed with ideas for bringing all ages together, not just for Palm Sunday and Easter Day but for the whole of the Easter period. This is not always easy, since the Easter story is very sad and harrowing in parts – and it may seem better to exclude younger children at certain points during our Easter worship. However, the resources in this book are designed to suggest ways of including children in everything, encouraging them to experience at their own level, both the sadness and the joy of this wonderful time of the Christian year.

There is plenty for everyone – whether you are looking for a school assembly, an all-age event, an all-age service or a short talk. In addition, there are Easter crafts, cookery, rhymes, songs and raps, puzzles, games and prayers. As a special feature, there are carefully crafted stories for younger children through which they can hear and understand the whole Easter story from Palm Sunday to Easter Sunday and beyond. The stories use different methods that involve the children, engaging all their senses. For any occasion on which you wish to help people think beyond Easter eggs and hot cross buns, look inside Easter Cracked for ideas to give meaning and depth to your celebration of this special time of the year.

There are fresh ideas for children and adults alike – those who are new to the Easter story and those who know it well. You might wish to have an evangelistic event for the families, or learn about the meaning of the cross in an all-age service. You might have the opportunity to take an assembly in school, or hold a children's event that has a serious purpose but is fun. You may be looking for additional resources to add into services and events you have already planned. Easter Cracked provides all this! We hope that you will enjoy dipping into the resources here, adapting them to your own situation so that people of all ages will learn to love Easter, get to know Jesus and understand what he did for all of us that very first Easter-time.

Some of the material in Easter Cracked has been written especially for this book, while other items are favourites from previous publications. We are grateful to all the writers for their contributions.

Christine Wright

Passover picnic

An event for younger children and their families

You will need: Passover food: hard-boiled egg, unleavened bread or Matzo crackers, watercress or parsley (representing hyssop), salt water, red grape juice or red fruit squash, stewed grated carrot and apple (as a substitute for haroseth, which is made with nuts), a large round platter

With any activity involving food, be aware of health, safety, hygiene and allergy issues. Find out from parents and carers beforehand if there are any food allergies or intolerances.

To help everyone appreciate the 'specialness' of the meal, provide decorated paper plates and brightly coloured napkins. Add something sweet like fruit or raisins to round off the meal. If eating indoors, lighting some candles would add to the atmosphere, but obviously put these well out of the children's reach.

Explain that Jesus and his friends shared a special meal just like this one and Jesus thanked God for the food. Say or sing a simple grace.

Give tiny samples of everything. (The traditional lamb and horseradish have been omitted in this version.) Encourage the children to taste everything. As you break the matzos and pour the juice, remind the children that Jesus wants us to remember him.

Remind everyone that at the end of their special meal, Jesus and his friends sang a song. Sing a praise song together as you finish.

Celebration meal

A low-key evangelistic event for families by John Hattam

Let CS Lewis' *The Lion, the Witch and the Wardrobe* provide a way in to the meaning of Easter. Watch the film and end with a celebration meal.

The aim: To help people of all ages to engage with the Easter narrative, allowing the allegory of the film story to shed light on the meaning of the Scripture passages.

Preparation: Prepare place settings in advance, with an eye for graphics and good presentation. The place settings for adults include the words of Ephesians 2:1–10. For children, use a resurrection scene which they can colour when they have finished eating but the adults have not! Supply plenty of felt-tip pens.

Have some booklets ready for handing out. Suggested booklets are: for adults, *What's the point?* Norman Warren, Lion; for under-7s, *Friends with Jesus*, Scripture Union; for 8 to 9s, *Me+Jesus*, Scripture Union; for 10 to 12s, *Jesus=friendship forever*, Scripture Union; for young people, *Big Questions about You and God*, David Lawrence, Scripture Union. Allow the booklet to do the talking! However, think through some prayerful, sensitive follow-up.

Prepare some A4 cards, enough for everyone to be able to see one. Make sure you have a dice for each table. Write the following words on the front of the card:

Snow reminds me of the time when...
What makes Christmas special for you?
Imagine what it would be like for it always to be winter and never Christmas.
What do you think is going to happen when Lucy returns to the house through the wardrobe?
Narnia in winter could represent... (Children can ask an adult to help finish this sentence.)

On the reverse side of the cards, draw boxes with the following words inside:

Box 1

'We are people of flesh and blood. That is why Jesus became one of us. He died to destroy the devil, who had power over death.'
Hebrews 2:14

Box 2

'God loved the people of this world so much that he gave his only Son, so that everyone who has faith in him will have eternal life and never really die.'
John 3:16

Food: This is eaten in three stages, the real feasting and party poppers being reserved for the final stage, after the end of the film. You could provide all the food yourself, or ask guests to bring some celebration food for the main meal (to be eaten cold). Form people into groups or 'tables'. Serve the main meal immediately after the end of the film. Have 'nibbles' to eat during the showing of the film (see below). Cover these eats with a cloth.

The film: This meal uses the BBC Family Classics Series (DVD and Video, running time 165 minutes) version of the story. There are other versions available, including a short cartoon version from STL (DVD and Video, running time 95 minutes). *The Chronicles of Narnia: The Lion, the Witch and the Wardrobe* (Disney, released in cinemas in the UK December 2005) may be available, depending on when you do this event. Make sure your projection and sound are of good quality.

Start the film, and run it to the point where Lucy returns after having said goodbye to Tumnus the Faun.

Interval 1: Remove the table covering to reveal the 'nibbles'. Hand out the A4 cards with the questions on one side and have enough for everyone to be able to see one. Also provide a dice for each table. Read (or ask someone else to read) the words inside one of the 'boxes' on the other side the card. (It doesn't matter if the same words are read more than once.)

To play the game, take it in turns to throw the dice. If you throw a '1', answer question 1; throw a '2' and answer question 2 and so on. Speak for no longer than one minute. Say 'pass' if you can't think of anything to say! Everyone helps themselves to a nibble after each throw.

Allow maximum 10–12 minutes for this interval, and then restart the film.

Interval 2: Stop the film at the stone-table incident as Aslan dies.

Celebration meal

Ask everyone to be still for the next few moments. Explain that the film has paused for a few minutes at a serious place in the story. The end is not far away, when the celebration meal will begin. But for a few moments, listen to an account of another execution, from Luke 23:32–43, Mark 10:45, John 10:17–18.

Choose two or three people, male or female, who can read with dramatic effect. (They should practise thoroughly beforehand.) Have a good PA system so that when the readers drop their voices, they can still be clearly heard. The readings could be supplemented with good-quality crucifixion images via PowerPoint and/or music.

Make this as brief an interval as is necessary to allow, perhaps, for a 'comfort stop' as well as the readings. Resume the showing of the film to the end.

The main meal: Invite each table to set out their celebration meal and eat it!

Farewell: Avoid a speaker prolonging the event with an 'epilogue' saying: 'The meaning of the film is...' Your target audience may be expecting this, so give them a pleasant surprise by omitting it! Instead, say briefly, that as they will have realised, hidden behind the story of Aslan is another death and resurrection story which isn't fiction! Christians would like to tell the world that Jesus is alive, and he is the only one who offers forgiveness and new life to those who will come to him. But sometimes we need time and space to think through such claims and so rather than saying any more now, you would like everyone to accept a booklet to take home and read at leisure.

Cracking Easter

A presentation for junior school children by Wayne Dixon and Jem Sewell

This presentation was originally an Easter presentation one and a half hours long for Year 6 pupils, devised by Scripture Union schools' worker Wayne Dixon and Jem Sewell of Slough Baptist Church. This is a brief outline of the event, but if you would like more information on running an event like this in your church, please contact either Wayne Dixon or Jem Sewell at Slough Baptist Church on (UK) 01753 523058 or email WayneD@scriptureunion.org.uk or Jem@slough.baptistch.net

Preparation

Write to the schools you are asking to participate in January to give them time to fit the presentation into their schedule. Give details of how long the event will last and what will be happening. These invitations are more likely to succeed if they are built on already-existing positive relationships and personal contact.

Be aware of the ethnic and faith backgrounds of the children you are coming into contact with. This must be taken into account when talking about Easter, as some children will have affiliations to other religions. It may be worth taking advice from teachers on ways of handling this. Children will need to opt in to the session and parents will have to sign a consent form.

You need to make sure that your church is a secure place for the children to come to. Check that the building will be warm, that the toilets are safe and clean and that everybody involved has been CRB-checked. One person will need to be on the door as people arrive and stay there to ensure that the door is secured.

You will need

A booklet (already made up) for each child (see below); five or six story boards describing the key events of Holy Week, put up around the church; four eggs to be hidden around the church for the Easter egg hunt, each containing a clue (Clue 1: Where is the body of Jesus? Clue 2: The disciples changed as a result. Clue 3: There were more than 500 witnesses who saw Jesus alive. Clue 4: People still change as a result of believing that Jesus is alive.); chocolate Easter eggs to distribute.

The programme could include:

1 Welcome and introduction.
2 Catchphrase quiz with two teams on an Easter theme.
3 Distribution of booklets and pencils.
4 Symbols we use today – helping the children understand the use of symbols in everyday life and connecting this with Christian symbols.
5 Presentation: a brief biography of Jesus in the four Gospels until the Palm Sunday accounts, perhaps told dramatically.
6 'Action on Palm Sunday': dramatic entry of dressed-up 'local' describing the events of Palm Sunday (for sample script see page 12).
7 Discovery time: time for the children to go around the church to look at the story boards. There should be space in the booklet to record the sequence of events. Children who finish this activity early could do the wordsearch in the booklet, or draw a design for a cross.
8 Summary of the pictures and story boards (all together).
9 Evidence for the resurrection combined with an Easter egg hunt game.
10 Easter remembered: this section could be done in two groups, one learning about traditions and practices associated with Easter; the other learning how Holy Communion and baptism serve as a reminder of the resurrection. The groups change around after ten minutes.
11 The Easter Rap: learning and performing an Easter Rap.
12 Questions, conclusion and distribute chocolate.

Example of a letter sent to schools in Slough.

24 January 2005

SLOUGH BAPTIST CHURCH
Welcome Witness Worship

Dear R.E. Co-ordinator /Year 6 Teachers

The Easter Story – An event for Year 6

Following the success of our Christmas presentation, we are once again running our Easter event "The Easter Story".

The presentations will take place mornings and afternoons from Monday 7 March until Friday 11 March. Timings are given on the enclosed booking slip.

We are able to offer assistance with travel - up to 20% of the price of your coach booking for the trips to and from church – please ask for details. This presentation will need to be undertaken at the church as we will be demonstrating Baptism; in our tradition Baptism is by full immersion, and we just can't transport that much water!

May we encourage you to book early as last year's presentations were over subscribed; bookings will be taken on a first come first served basis.

We hope that again all chocolate will be sponsored by Mars Confectionery and we look forward to your help in eating their generosity!

Yours sincerely

Jem Sewell
Jem Sewell
Pastor

Wayne Dixon
Wayne Dixon
Scripture Union Schools' Worker
Slough, Windsor and Maidenhead

What the teachers said last year :

"Brilliant as usual! The children really enjoyed the Christmas presentation and were very excited about coming back today for the Easter presentation."

"Children were engaged and asked lots of questions, especially when reading the Easter Story. Thanks again."

"... brought Easter alive in a child-friendly way, particularly to children who have other beliefs."

"An excellent presentation of the Easter Story – always difficult to teach. With lots of fast pacy sections captivating the children's interest."

Slough Baptist Church
Windsor Road, Slough
Berkshire, SL1 2EJ

Tel: 01753 523058
Fax: 01753 572418

email: office@slough.baptistch.net
website: www.slough.baptistch.net

Pastors: Jem Sewell
David Warren

Secretary: Rupert Scott
Treasurer: John Shepherd

Data Protection Act: The Diaconate is the Data Controller for the purposes of the Act and personal data may be processed for general church purposes

Cracking Easter

Content of booklets

These booklets can have any number of quizzes, wordsearches or puzzles in them to give the children something quick to do. Make them as visual as possible and leave plenty of room for the children to write in, where required. Consult a teacher when compiling the booklet if you don't have expertise in teaching this age-group. The following items are essential parts of the booklets, as they'll be discussed from the front.

Symbols we use today

Text: Easter is fun, but it can sometimes be confusing. For some people it is only a holiday, and for others the Christian festival of Easter uses a lot of symbols they may not understand. But we all use symbols a lot! What do these symbols stand for?

(You could include the logos of some well-known companies, other symbols giving directions or information and a cross. Leave room for children to write the answers beside each symbol.)

The Easter story told

Text: In the Bible there are four accounts of the Easter story, each written by a different person. Normally when writing a biography of someone famous, you look mainly at their life. When we look at the amount of space given by these four writers to the death of Jesus, it must have seemed pretty important to them.

Percentage of book focusing on the last week of Jesus' life:
Matthew 10%
Mark 20%
Luke 15%
John 40%

This is how John finishes his biography of Jesus:

> 'Jesus did many other things. If they were all written in books, I don't suppose there would be room enough in the whole world for all the books.'

We have lots of evidence that Jesus lived in Israel and died on a cross about 2,000 years ago. As well as all the writing in the Bible, other historians around at the same time as Jesus, who were not Christians, have written about him.

The Easter Miracle

What evidence was found for the resurrection?

Write down four clues in the boxes below.

Easter remembered

1 The cross
The cross was a device, invented by the Romans, for killing criminals. It was such a horrible way of dying that no Roman citizen was allowed to be killed in that way. Because Jesus was killed on a cross, Christians ever since have used the cross as a symbol of what God has done for them through Jesus.

2 Communion
All Christians believe that Communion is very important. The basic symbols are bread and wine. Jesus used a Jewish festival called *Passover* and gave it a new meaning for Christians.

The Easter story board

Inlcude pictures in order, similar to those on the story boards around the church. Beside each picture, put a box in which to write the event to which the picture refers.

Modern traditions

Include this quiz for the children to do:

1 Which animal has the mark of a cross on its back?
a) Lion b) Tiger **c) Donkey**

2 Which bird produces the largest egg?
a) Ostrich b) Eagle c) Parrot

3 What substance makes up 80% of an egg?
a) Yolk **b) Water** c) Shell

4 What is the earliest date Easter can be?
a) 8 April b) 10 March **c) 22 March**

5 On what day did Jesus come back to life?
a) Good Friday b) Palm Sunday
c) Easter Sunday

6 The custom of giving eggs can be traced back to China in...
a) 900 BC b) 150 BC c) 70 AD

7 What was the price of Thornton's most expensive Easter egg last year?
[This changes every year – use the most recent price, plus two other options.]

8 How many Crème Eggs do Cadbury's make in an hour?
a) 6,000 **b) 66,000** c) 600

9 Rearrange the letters EASTER to make another six letter word!

Easter events

Easter wordsearch

Include a wordsearch in the booklet. There is a giant one you can use on page 80, if you can cram it in!

Easter rap

There is a rap on pages 89 and 90 which you may like to include in the book, depending on how much space there is. Raps always go down well with children of this age. So, no matter how self-conscious you may feel performing them, as long as you perform them whole-heartedly, they will be appreciated! They will go down even better if you have backing tracks, actions and ways for the group to join in!

Other material

It would also be good to include in the booklet some fun Easter facts, the answers to the questions (but in an unobtrusive place) and some contact details for your church.

Script for 'Action on Palm Sunday'

This monologue is told from the point of view of an eye-witness at Jesus' Palm Sunday entrance into Jerusalem.

The eye witness enters in costume, excitedly.

There I was, going about my usual business on Sunday afternoon and there was... there was a buzz about the place.

Now I knew it was Celebration Time and many people were coming together to remember our festival of Passover. That was important...

Then it happened! Loads of people were out on the streets, shouting and singing and screaming. It was an amazing carnival atmosphere. Let me tell you what they were doing. Some of them were breaking off palm branches and laying them on the ground. Others were taking off their coats and laying them on the ground. 'What was going on?' I thought.

Then, in the distance I could see this figure of a man sitting on a donkey, cruising into town. As the man got closer I could recognise him. It was Jesus!! Jesus the Carpenter. Jesus, who had been travelling around saying some amazing things and doing some incredible things.

Yet now here he is coming into Jerusalem, as calm as you like, sitting on a donkey. Now I happen to know that a donkey is an animal that represents peace. Jesus certainly looked peaceful whilst all around him were going crazy with excitement.

As I listened, I got the gist of what the crowd were shouting. It was 'Praise God! Praise God! Bless him who comes in the name of the Lord!'

Man, it was quite a sight. It was amazing. I've never experienced anything like this before. Yet amongst all this, Jesus remained cool and calm – as if he knew exactly what he was about to do and what would happen next.

Then Jesus just got off his donkey and went straight into the temple – and events carried on from there.

Do you want to know what happened next? Well, just watch this space. Anyway, I thought I must just tell you this – it was the start of an amazing week. It was no ordinary day. See you! (Run off excitedly.)

Easter corners

A meditation for children, following the events of Holy Week

Easter corners involves a lot of effort, but it does give children the opportunity to be in a small group and to focus on several Bible stories and themes. If you only have a small number of children, you can, of course, omit some of the corners.

Preparation

Have one area for meeting all together, where the children can sit and stand comfortably. Decorate this area with large leafy plants, to represent a roadside with palm trees. You could include some 'rocks' and lighting effects – bright sunlight for Palm Sunday and soft dawn light for Easter morning. Later, for the end of the session, add flowers, to indicate a garden, and rearrange the area slightly to indicate a different place.

Have some tables at the side with felt-tip pens and crayons. These will be used for the children who come early, but make sure that you have a simple activity (drawing or colouring) available in case any opt out of the corners. Also have a 'listening ear' available here throughout the session for children who want someone to talk to.

Around the room, or in other rooms close by, set up five 'corners'. These are displays with sitting space and interactive items for a group of children. Make them look as authentic as possible, ie use wooden, not metal furniture, and any items of clothing or equipment should be biblical in style. You will need at least one leader in each corner, and others to take the groups from corner to corner. Having a 'time manager' is essential. He or she will indicate when to move from one corner to the next.

The displays should include:

Corner 1 – Jesus in the temple
- An upturned table and stool
- A length of rope or leather
- Coins and feathers strewn around
- A cage or basket suitable for a small animal

For the activity: double paper hearts, linked at the top; drawing/writing materials, including red crayons

Corner 2 – Jesus and the precious perfume
- A low table covered with a rich cloth
- A lounging place, eg a blanket and cushions (these should be luxurious/ornamental)
- 'Silver' dishes, perhaps with fruit such as oranges, pomegranates, dates and grapes

- An ornate bottle
- If possible, also include something sweet-smelling here such as pot pourri, a room freshener or, if safe, a scented candle

For the activity: bottle-shaped papers, drawing/writing materials

Corner 3 – Jesus at the Last Supper
- A low table and lounging place as before, but simple rather than rich
- A plain wooden platter with flat bread such as pitta or Nan on it
- A pottery or wooden goblet
- A jug containing red grape juice or blackcurrant squash

For the activity: paper cups, paper plates, brown and purple paper, labels, scissors, glue sticks, drawing/writing materials

Corner 4 – Jesus washes his disciples' feet
- A large (not plastic) bowl and jug (the jug could be tipped on its side in the bowl with clear glass pebbles tipping out, to look like drops of water)
- A towel

For the activity: papers, scissors, drawing and writing materials

Corner 5 – Jesus dies on the cross
- A large plain cross
- Items such as a wooden mallet, nails, dice, a purple cloak/cloth, a crown of thorns, a notice saying 'This is the King of the Jews'
- A plain white cloth, eg tablecloth or sheet

For the activity: small papers, backing paper, glue sticks, black paper cross, gel pens, cross bookmarks, drawing/writing materials

Beginning the session:

As the children come in they are given an A4 envelope, to write their name on (and decorate if there is time). They are going to collect the activities in the envelope as they move around the corners.

Introduction

Gather the children in your main area. Explain to them that they are going to hear the story of what happened to a man called Jesus during the last week of his life. We are going to imagine that we are with Jesus, watching what happens.

Narration

So where are we now? We are on a hot dusty road in Jerusalem. There is some shade from the palm trees around, but otherwise the sun is very bright. Why is there such a crowd here? And what is all that shouting in the distance? Oh, somebody says Jesus is coming! You have heard of this special man. You have heard that he can do wonderful things like making blind people see and lame people walk again. He welcomes everybody, even children, and entertains them with stories that really make you think. Many people think he is the man sent by God to save the Jewish nation from the Romans. No wonder there is cheering and shouting. And here he comes now! People are throwing their cloaks on the floor for his donkey to walk on, and breaking branches off the palm trees to wave in the air.

Sing a lively song such as 'We want to see Jesus lifted high' to represent Palm Sunday.

Divide the children into groups according to age or, if your numbers are small enough, stay in one group. Unless you have other activities arranged so that you can stagger the children's starting times, let the youngest children visit the corners in the right order and explain to the older ones, who are visiting them in the wrong order, the timing of each event as they come to it. Make sure there is time in each corner for quiet thought and questions from the children, as well as the activity.

Corner 1: In the temple

Matthew 21:12–17

Narration

After Jesus has ridden into Jerusalem on the donkey, he has come to the temple. This is the huge building where the Jews come to worship God. Some of it we aren't allowed to go in as it is so special, but this bit is all right. This is the place where people meet, and where they buy the things they need to worship God. It is noisy because there are animals here – lambs and goats and pigeons – waiting to be bought and sacrificed. Jesus doesn't mind the noise. But what he *does* mind is the cheating that is going on. The people have to change their money into 'temple money' and the merchants are making a profit out of it. They are not there to help people to worship God; they are just lying and cheating and making money. Jesus is

furious. Look, he has picked up a piece of rope, and he's whipping the ground with it. He's pushing over the tables. All the money is spilling to the ground. 'You've made God's house a den of thieves!' he is shouting.

Some sick people have discovered that Jesus is in the temple and they have come to find him. He touches them and they become well. We and the other children are watching with delight. 'Hooray for Jesus!' we shout.

But who's coming here with faces like thunder? It's the priests and teachers who work in the temple. We hide behind a pillar to see what they will say. To our surprise they seem quite happy with the cheating, but they tell Jesus off for doing good things like making people better, and for letting us shout hooray.

If you wish, read the story from the Bible.

Questions
Who do you think was doing what God wanted in his temple?
What was wrong about some of the things going on?
Jesus knew that it is what is in people's hearts that is important. Doing the right thing on the outside is not enough.

Activity
Give the children a folded heart. They can colour the outside red. Inside, they can write or draw some of the things that are important to them. Ask them to think what Jesus would feel about what is in their hearts.

Corner 2: Jesus is anointed at Bethany

John 12:1–8

Narration
Jesus has done something wonderful for the family who live here. Lazarus had died and was buried in a cave, but four days later Jesus called him back to life. Lazarus and his sisters, Martha and Mary, have invited Jesus to a celebratory meal. Everything is as special as they can make it – the best dishes, the best cloth, and Martha made sure there was also the best food. But Mary wanted to do something even more special.

Read or tell the story from John 12:1–8.

Easter corners

Questions

Why do you think Mary wanted to do something so special for Jesus?

What would you want to do for someone who had brought your brother/sister/parent back to life?

Activity

Give the children time to answer or to think quietly. Give out bottle-shaped papers. Ask the children to draw or write about 'something that is precious to me' and to think whether there is something special they might do with it.

Corner 3: Jesus at the Last Supper

Luke 22:14–20

Narration

Once a year everybody celebrated a special feast called the Passover. It reminded them of how God had saved his people long ago. They had roast lamb and drank wine. It was a very happy time. Jesus and his friends have come on Thursday evening to this upstairs room to enjoy their feast together. But it isn't as happy as it has been before. Jesus seems to be in a very serious mood. Well, there are people out there who hate him. They think he is a troublemaker, especially after all those crowds cheering him on Sunday. And some of his friends think Jesus isn't doing anything to help himself. Why doesn't he quietly leave Jerusalem while he can?

But Jesus knows this isn't what God wants. He knows his enemies will arrest him and he will be killed. But he is going to die on behalf of everyone, everyone in the whole world. Jesus gives his friends a picture of this. He breaks bread and shares it amongst them. 'My body will be broken for you,' he says. He pours out wine. 'My blood will be poured out for you.' His friends didn't understand then, and perhaps you don't really understand it all at the moment, but just listen to the story.

Read or tell the story from Luke 22:14–20. At the appropriate times offer the children a small piece of bread and a little grape juice or blackcurrant drink (make sure they know this represents wine made from grapes) in the paper cups.

Questions

What would you want Jesus to explain to you about what he did at the supper?

Activity

Give the children time to think quietly and ask any questions. Ask them to cut out bread and grape shapes and paste them on cardboard plates to remind them of the story.

Corner 4: Jesus washes his disciples' feet

John 13:3–17

Narration

Remind the children of the first activity, where they were imagining they were on a hot dusty road. What would their feet be like? Dirty and sweaty! How lovely to have them washed in cool water! A good host would make sure there was someone to do this, but when it was just you and your friends, one of you had to volunteer. It isn't a job anybody likes, so no one has offered to do it. While we are eating our supper on the Thursday night, Jesus picks up a towel, ties it round his waist, and starts to wash his friends' feet.

Read or tell the story from John 13:3–17. If you have time, ask for a volunteer to have their feet washed as the story is told. Make sure the atmosphere is kept quiet and reverent.

Questions

Why do you think Jesus washed his friends' feet? What could you do for people to show them you loved them?

If Jesus could wash you, what would you want him to make clean? (Omit this question for younger children.)

Activity

Ask the children to draw round one foot and cut it out. On one side, they draw or write about 'what I could do for someone to show love to them'. On the other side, they write or draw about Jesus washing them clean.

Corner 5: Jesus dies on the cross

Luke 23:32–47

Narration

After our supper on the Thursday night, Jesus and his friends have come to an olive orchard. Jesus is frightened, because he knows what God wants him to do. He prays that God will help him. When his enemies come into the orchard, Jesus is ready to be arrested. They take him away, beat him up and tell lies about him. They want to be rid of him once and for all, so they make sure the Roman soldiers take him off to be nailed to a cross of wood, until he dies. Then his friends take his body down carefully and wrap it in a clean white cloth (demonstrate with your cloth). They put it in a cave tomb on Friday afternoon.

Read or tell the story from Luke 23:32–47.

Questions
Dying on a cross is what happened to very bad men, and Jesus wasn't a bad man. In fact, he was the only truly good man who ever lived. Why do you think Jesus had to die? (Allow the children to say freely what they think.)

Activity
Ask the children to think about any wrong things they have ever done. Invite them to draw or write about them (they can just draw marks or symbols to represent the wrong things if they would rather) on small pieces of paper and paste them on the backing paper or, if the group is small enough, draw them straight on to the backing paper. Look at the paper. This represents all the wrong things we have ever done. Jesus had never done any of those, but we have. What happened when this perfect man died on the cross? Paste a large cross over the paper. The cross has crossed out our sins! Jesus died instead of us.

Read Romans 5:8.

Allow time for the children to think and ask questions. Then, if you think it is appropriate, let the children write words of praise on the cross with gold/silver pens.

Give the children a cross-shaped bookmark to take away.

All together

Gather the children together again in your central area. Show the folded cloth and remind them that on Friday evening Jesus' body was laid in the tomb in a garden. It was all done in rather a hurry, and a huge stone was put across the entrance as a door.

Narration
Jesus was dead. We know that he died to take away the bad things that we have done, but how were his friends ever going to find that out?

The next day was Saturday, their holy day, so no one was allowed to visit the tomb. But as early as possible on the Sunday some women are coming to the garden bringing sweet-smelling spices. They want to finish making Jesus' body as nice as possible. We will go with them. It is barely light and we can't see very well. Then we have a dreadful thought. What about that huge stone? There is no way we can push that out of the way. But now we are arriving at the garden. What is that bright light? And that great big hole? An angel is sitting on the stone and the tomb is empty! 'He has risen from the dead!' says the angel.

Now we know that Jesus really did take away our bad things when he died on the cross. God has proved it by raising Jesus to life!

Sing a joyful song representing Easter day. Finish with a prayer appropriate to your group of children.

If possible, have time at the end, perhaps while another craft activity is available or refreshments are served, for children to be able to talk further if they wish.

Bread for the world

Worship for early Easter morning

You will need: tea, coffee and fruit juice; a collection of bread from many lands; flatbread and wine/fruit juice; candles, if possible

Although many of the breads can be bought in the shops, it is fun to make some types beforehand. Indeed this could become part of the worship, as you consider what Jesus meant by saying, 'I am the bread that gives life!' (John 6:35a). Here are some ideas:

Tortillas (Mexico)
Nan (India)
Chapattis (India)
Parathas (Pakistan and India)
Pitta bread (Greece)
Hot cross buns (England)
Pane di Pasqua (Italy)
Kulichi (Russia)
Rye bread (Russia)
Ciabatta (Italy)

Kulichi

The Kulich is a cylindrical dome-shaped bread which is only baked once a year and is blessed in a ceremony at church on the Saturday preceding Easter Sunday. For the Easter feast, a dark orange beeswax candle is stuck in the top and lit before the celebration starts.

This worship activity is designed for use early on Easter morning and could start as early as 5.30 or 6 in the morning! If the weather is good and the eastern horizon is visible from near where you are meeting, you might include a time to go out and watch the sunrise as part of the session.

Activity outline

Welcome

Welcome everyone to the worship activity and thank them for coming out so early in the morning! Make sure everyone has a drink if they want one. Wish everyone a happy Easter. Your church tradition may have an appropriate response which you could say at this point.

Poem – 'Arboretum'

Read out this poem as a reminder of the Easter story so far:

Trees by the wayside, their branches raised high,
Uplifted by children; 'Hosanna!' they cry.
Green leaves waved in praise
As the King passes by.

Trees in the olive grove – night full of fears;
Where shadow meets darkness, all evil

disappears.
But the battle is won
As the King prays in tears.

Trees from the wasteland – a bough roughly torn,
Made into a circle of sharp twisted thorn.
In suffering glory
A King's crown is worn
Trees on the hill, against lowering skies,
Where the dark tries to hide a man's agonised cries,
And God's face turned away
From the King as he dies.

Trees in the garden, with blossoms that sing,
With all nature and angels, that death could not cling.
The tomb is quite empty.
He is risen – the King!

© Marjory Francis

Reading 1
John 6:35-37

Response

Share the bread around and in smaller groups ask everyone to consider, while they are eating, what they think Jesus meant by saying, 'I am the bread that gives life!' Ask people to be honest about what they think. Make sure people understand that they can say they don't know, if they're not sure what Jesus meant. Allow some time for discussion. If you like, you could ask the groups to feed back.

Reading 2
Matthew 28:1-10

Response

Celebrate communion as your church is accustomed to celebrating it, using a flat bread, rather than a loaf or roll.

Prayer

Ask each person or group to take a piece of bread from a different part of the world and pray for that place, that Jesus' life-giving sacrifice would be known in that country on this happy day. You might like to provide an information sheet on each country represented, so that people can pray more specifically. A wealth of information is available on the Internet.

Depart

Say the grace together. You might wish to have a special Easter breakfast together.

An outdoor meditation for Good Friday by John Grayston

Good Friday is one of the most significant days in the church calendar, but it is not easy to know how to approach it. Some church traditions see it as primarily a day of silent vigil, of remembering the pain of Jesus' death and identifying with the sense of loss and confusion that the disciples felt; this prepares the way for the joy and release of Easter Sunday. Others see it as a day to celebrate the victory of the cross.

For many outside the church, Good Friday has become indistinguishable from any other. There is little to remind them of God's love in Jesus, demonstrated in his death. It is unlikely that they will find their way to church on Good Friday, so we shall have to take the message out. And since on Good Friday we remember one who was visibly seen carrying his cross on the streets of Jerusalem this may be a time to go on the streets.

There are different approaches. In some towns, the churches organise a joint March of Witness or something similar, perhaps with a joint service. In others, groups from all the churches converge on the town centre from different directions, gradually meeting and joining like the tributaries of a river until three groups carrying crosses converge on the town centre and hold an open-air service. There are obvious advantages of a united event, but the ability to organise it depends on the size of the community and the relationships between churches. It is possible to do something on a smaller scale which can be equally effective.

Planning

Set objectives – what are you trying to achieve? Demonstrate the church is there? Encourage people to think about Easter? Pray for the neighbourhood? All of these and others will be valid, but your choice of objective will affect what you actually do. Bear in mind that most people will not immediately associate symbols like the cross with the heart of the Christian message, and if the main aim is evangelistic we may need to start further back.

Plan prayerfully with your objectives in mind. Think about the route. If you are going to pray for local activities, plan stops accordingly and brief people to pray. Alternatively, have short times of prayer and reflection at the places you've planned to stop. Organise different people to pray, or read from the Bible or other spiritual writing. If you plan to stop for times of worship and reflection, plan these around the Passion narrative. Organise readings and songs. Perhaps in advance, ask various groups or families in the church to prepare a banner or poster which could act as a backdrop. If you have talented dramatists, think about including a short drama.

You may wish to have suitable pieces of literature to hand out – a Gospel in a modern translation, a selection of scriptures, a leaflet explaining the Christian message, or introducing your church. Some you will need to obtain; others can be produced locally. You might want to link it with a distribution of the 'Jesus' film or a showing of the film in the church or some neutral venue (the 'Jesus' film is distributed by Agapé: 0121 683 5090 or sales@agape.org.uk).

Give people things to meditate on between stops, perhaps on paper. If there are children, ensure that they have something to help them focus on the message – pictures, conversations, appropriate songs, depending on the mix and the age. Avoid a situation where people have little to think about and walk along chatting about anything and nothing.

Think about safety aspects. Liase with the local police over the route and have marshals in safety jackets at the back and sides of the group.

Good Friday walk

Sample programme

This is based on a particular community and will need to be adapted to fit in with your own area.

10.00	Meet at the church. Read Mark 14:32-42. Pray that you will be faithful in standing with Jesus and witnessing for him. Sing an appropriate song - possibly the Taize chant, 'Watch and pray'. Spend time in silence thinking of Jesus in the Garden. Have a prayer of thanksgiving for Jesus' obedience to the Father.
10.15	Move off, walk to the local doctor's surgery. Read Mark 14:43-65. Thank God for the steadfast love of Jesus. Pray for those who care for others in the community.
10.25	Walk to the prison. Read Mark 14:66 - 15:15. Remember that Jesus went through arrest, trial and unjust sentence so that we might be free. Pray for justice in the world, for lawmakers and those who enforce the law, for prisoners and those who work with them.
10.35	On the green in the middle of a housing estate. Read Mark 15:16-41. In silence think about Jesus' death. Then, noticing the division between those who believe and those who don't, pray for those who live and work in your community that they might come to see that Jesus really is the Son of God.
10.45	Outside the Primary School. Read Mark 15:42-47. Reflect at this point on the love shown by others for Jesus and then pray for those who care for others in your community. Pray for schools, for the education system and for children and young people generally.
10.55	Return to base. Close with a short act of worship which might include songs and further readings - Romans 5:1-11 or Isaiah 52:12 - 53:12 are worth considering - and prayers for any other area of the community you have missed. Close the meditation by reading Romans 8:1-5 or 1 John 4:1-7, and dismissing people with an appropriate blessing.

Suggestions for hymns and songs: 'Alas and did my Saviour bleed'; 'Come and see'; 'Glory be to Jesus, who in bitter pains'; 'He was pierced'; 'Here is love vast as the ocean'; 'His hands were pierced'; 'How deep the Father's love for us'; 'It is a thing most wonderful'; 'It's your blood'; 'Man of Sorrows what a name'; 'My song is love unknown'; 'O sacred head surrounded'; 'Thank you for the cross'; 'The cross has said it all'; 'The price is paid'; 'There is a green hill'; 'When I survey the wondrous cross'

What are kings like?

A short talk for Palm Sunday by Mary Hawes

You will need: some 'kingly' props – a crown, a toy car, a royal robe (possibly a cloak) and a chair decorated as a throne

The talk: Say that a king is special, and ask what it might be like to be a king. Elicit the idea that kings are usually very privileged people. They have the power to rule over their kingdom and tell people what to do. They live in palaces and have people to serve them; wherever they go they are given special treatment. Ask for a volunteer to come and receive some royal treatment. Using suitable words, place the crown on their head, the robe around their shoulders, give them the car for transport and sit them on the throne. Then invite the congregation to cheer 'Long live King (Queen) X!'

Remind everyone about the crowds who cheered Jesus. They thought that he was coming to be their earthly king, the king of the Jews, ruling over them and setting them free from the Romans who occupied their country. They wanted to give him the royal treatment! They wanted Jesus to show his power by overthrowing their enemies.

Jesus wasn't an earthly king. *(Take away the volunteer's car.)* He didn't have fancy transport – he rode on a borrowed donkey, the sign of God's heavenly king (Zechariah 9:9). *(Take away the royal robe.)* Jesus didn't wear royal robes – he wore ordinary clothes, sometimes even the clothes of a servant (John 13:2–5). *(Take away the crown.)* Jesus didn't wear a golden crown. Instead, when the crowd turned against him for not being an earthly king, they made him wear a crown of thorns.

So what sort of king is Jesus?

A king to bring us close to God. God sent Jesus to be his king here on earth, so that we could get to know God. No other king can do that for us.

A king who loves us. Jesus loves and knows each one of us. No other king can do that.

A king who shows us the way. Throughout his life, by his words and actions, King Jesus showed us the way to God and the way that God wants us to live. No other king can do that.

A king like Jesus deserves our love and praise. He deserves to be welcomed into each of our lives.

A meal to remember

An explanation of the Last Supper by Tracey Wheeler

Preparation: load a table with items associated with special meals, eg food, drink, plates, party poppers, cups, presents, candlesticks and crackers. In the middle have a simple cup of wine and loaf of bread, almost hidden. If appropriate to your tradition, these activities will be effective as part of a Communion service.

The talk: Talk about special meals and the events they mark, eg birthday, wedding, Christmas, retirement. What is special and enjoyable about such meals? Point out the relevant items on the table.

Explain how these meals help us to remember what we are celebrating, eg singing 'Happy Birthday' is a reminder that the birthday person is special.

Special meals help us remember and mark important events. The meal Jesus shared with his friends (recorded in Matthew 26:17–30) marked the most important event ever. Let's see how.

A remembering meal
Refer to today's 'remembering meals', eg a birthday. Passover looked back to the rescue from Egypt. But, by mentioning 'covenant' – God's special relationship with his people – Jesus looks back to all God had done in the Old Testament: his big plan. Give a quick overview: God created people to share a perfect life with him; people rejected that; *(Start to remove items from table.)* God chose a nation to be specially his, rescued them, told them how to live as he wanted in his Promised Land; they kept turning their backs on his plan; God kept bringing them back to him. The whole point of the plan was, at the right time, to send his Son. Now here was God's Son celebrating this meal. This was not just a nice time together. It was about something very important. *(Remove frivolous items.)*

A lonely meal
Jesus was sharing with his disciples. Give a personal example of enjoying a shared celebratory meal. But Jesus' words show that he will soon be alone – one of them will betray him

Short talks

(vs 21–25). The rest will desert him (vs 31–35) – their courage and devotion to him will not be great enough. What Jesus was about to do, what the meal was all about, was something he had to do alone. Only he could do it. *(Remove several items.)*

A sad meal

Jesus used the bread and wine, part of the Passover meal, to explain that his body was about to be broken and his blood shed (vs 26–28). He was about to die, but it would not be an accident or the defeat of God's plan. It was something deliberate – the heart of God's plan. *(Remove the last few items, leaving just the cup and bread on the table.)*

A happy and 'looking forward' meal

Jesus says that his death will bring about a new relationship with God (vs 27–29), with sins forgiven. What could be happier? It is a celebration meal after all. It is not only for Jesus' friends, but for many more people (v 28). Jesus will rise again (v 32) and he looks forward to life with his many friends in the future – a feast in God's kingdom.

Jesus invites us too. He wants us to receive all the good things he has achieved for us by his death. Illustrate with 'party bags' full of goodies, taken home from a special meal by everyone. (The bags could have words like 'new life', 'forgiveness', 'Jesus with us', 'with him for ever', 'rescue', 'promise', 'love', 'peace' written on them.)

Following Jesus' example

A talk suitable for a Good Friday service by Tracey Wheeler

Ask four people to read the key lines as outlined in the talk. You could also display pictures of Judas, the disciples, Peter, Pilate and a back view of Jesus, head bowed (see page 23).

Ask everyone to imagine a situation where you are suffering for being Christians (or refer to a real past or present situation), for example, if changing religion was illegal; your building has been closed; two church leaders have been arrested for being Christians. How might we react? Would we be tempted to do one of the following? (If you are using pictures, put these up for each character in turn.)

Betray those we love and look after ourselves –

like Judas. *(Reader 1: 'How much will you give me if I help you arrest Jesus?')*

Run away – like most of the disciples. *(Reader 2: 'All Jesus' disciples left him and ran away.')*

Hide the truth – like Peter. *(Reader 3: 'I don't know that man!')*

Give in to pressure – like Pilate. *(Reader 4: 'I won't have anything to do with killing this man. You are the ones doing it!')*

(Display the picture of Jesus.) We can never understand all Jesus went through. But we have heard something of how he responded to those who arrested, betrayed, tried and insulted him. He was overwhelmed with anguish and even fear; angry at the disciples' failure to stay awake with him; desperate to see if there might be another way; frustrated at his treatment by those arresting him. He was fully human as well as being God's Son.

But through it all his choice was for God, for God's ways and God's plan. He kept his eyes fixed on that. And he did it for us.

If suffering Christians keep their eyes fixed on Jesus, what does that mean?

Instead of looking after themselves, they care about God first. *(Reader 1: 'But do what you want, and not what I want.')*

Instead of running away, they stay and see it through. *(Reader 2: 'My Father, if there is no other way, and I must suffer, I will still do what you want.')*

Instead of hiding the truth, they speak out for what is right. *(Reader 3: 'Soon you will see the Son of Man sitting at the right side of God All-Powerful and coming on the clouds of heaven.')*

Instead of going with the crowd, they live for what God wants. *(Reader 4: 'But all this happened, so that what the prophets wrote would come true.')*

God still has a plan for his world – and a part for us to play in it. So we too have a choice, one that we must make every day (see Matthew 16:24). We need to start by acknowledging that God is in control. Like Jesus, we need to choose God's path by relying on his strength and keeping close to him through prayer.

Cross words

A short talk for Good Friday

Ask the children to write the word 'CROSS' down the side of a piece of paper. Then ask them to write the following words against each letter, one at a time, and discuss, in the group, what they mean:

Crucified (Jesus died)
Raised (God brought him to life again)
Our (Jesus can be 'ours' because he died for us)
Saviour (He saves us, because he died in our place)
Share (It is important to tell others about Jesus)

From hate to love

A short talk for Good Friday

You will need: paper (two contrasting colours), scissors, pens, sticky tape.

To prepare, cut nine squares of paper, all of the same colour and each measuring 7 cm in length. On each of the squares write one of these letters: H A T G I L O V E. Fold a sheet of paper in a contrasting colour in half lengthwise. Paste the letters, LOVE onto the folded paper. Take the letter T and put a piece of sticky tape across the top. Place the T over the existing letter V in such way that the sticky tape acts like a hinge. The letter T can now be lifted up to reveal the letter V underneath it. Over the letter O, hinge the letter I and, on top of that, the letter A. Over the letter L, hinge the letter G and ,on top of it, the letter H. Fold all the letters down to reveal the word HATE.

As you tell the following story, make the words in capitals appear on your visual aid.

The talk: There was so much HATE in the world that it made God very sad. He loved the people he had made, but how could he reach them and how could they reach him? God came up with a plan to create a GATE so people could pass through the barrier which was separating them from God. In this plan, God GAVE us his son Jesus to live as a real human being. Jesus was a teacher, a healer and a friend to the people he met. But the most important thing he did was to GIVE up his life. He died the most painful death imaginable. He did this so that you and I could LIVE. Jesus turned hate to LOVE!

Can you believe what you see?

A short talk for Easter-time by John Forrest

You will need: a flower bulb, packets of flour, margarine and sugar, a blank sheet of paper

The talk: Hold up the bulb and ask 'Can you believe this is something colourful and beautiful?' Hold up some flour, sugar and margarine and ask, 'Can you believe this will be a delicious cake?' Hold up the sheet of paper and ask, 'Can you believe this will be a wonderful painting?'

A wrinkled bulb, a few food ingredients and a blank sheet don't mean much in themselves, and yet we have an expectation that they will become something much more exciting. The expectation is based partly on our experience – we've seen it happen before.

But imagine you were seeing these objects for the first time. What would you need to see them as more than just plain objects?

First, you need information that something more is going to happen to them. Refer to the instructions that come with the bulb pack, and a recipe that explains how to make a cake.

Secondly, testimony from those who have seen something similar. You might talk to a gardener about the joys of waiting and seeing, or an artist who knows how to create a picture.

Thirdly, faith to believe that what is said will actually take place. You will have faith based on what you know and what you've heard, but ultimately it is up to you to decide where to place that faith.

Look at all the objects you have assembled – bulbs, cooking ingredients, paper. All of these are constant reminders of the life God has given us. They are reminders that there is new life available to all of us. God keeps on giving us reminders, and Easter Day reminds us of something about God which is vitally important: that Jesus is alive!

Short talks

Easter E G G

A talk for Easter Day, following a gospel reading about the resurrection, by John Forrest

Preparation: Prepare a large visual aid of an Easter egg. Make this from card. There should be three separate pieces which fit together to form an egg shape. (The centre piece should be a circle and the end pieces will be crescent shapes.) You should be able to join them together, either by pinning them up somewhere, or by having people hold them up in the right positions, or by having some joining rod behind them (eg a long piece of wood or a bamboo cane). Cover each piece with cheerful Easter wrapping paper and stick one large letter on each piece to spell EGG. It would also be useful to have an illustration of the empty tomb with the stone rolled back from the entrance.

The talk: Talk about Easter eggs. Ask who has had them, who likes them, what sort of eggs have people been getting this year. Explain that for some people, Easter means little more than chocolate eggs, but for Christians Easter means much more, and has almost *nothing* to do with chocolate eggs. Demonstrate by showing some of the differences.

Show the large egg you have prepared. Looking first at the visual aid as a chocolate egg, discuss what the letters could stand for, taking the 'egg' apart as you do so:

E could mean 'eager', 'ecstasy', 'everyone likes them'.
G (third letter) could mean 'gooey mess', 'groans when you've had too much'.
G (second letter) means 'gone', because eventually the egg disappears!

Hold on to the centre circle and explain that this is a link with the real Easter story. G starts the word 'gone'. Turn the circle round and show how it is a similar shape to the stone that was rolled in front of the tomb where Jesus' dead body was laid. An enormously heavy stone was put there to make sure the body stayed where it had been put. But the Easter story tells that the friends of Jesus found that the body had gone.

Put the egg together again, and suggest that it is entirely different to the chocolate version we thought about before.

E means 'everlasting'. Jesus showed through his resurrection that we may have everlasting life.
G (third letter) reminds us of the 'grave', but also that what Jesus did for us was 'good'.
G (second letter, centre circle) originally stood for 'gone' but, even more, thanks to what Jesus did, stands for 'God's glory'.

Judas

The disciples

Jesus

Peter

Pilate

Easter-time drama for younger children

You will need: simple costumes using material tied with ribbons, ties or scarves; or headgear: tinsel for angel, scarves for women, backwards baseball hats for guards, a traditional head cloth for Jesus and the priests, perfume pots, card or paper 'stone', tomb made of table or chairs covered in material, sound effects (eg gong, drum, saucepan lids), money bags.

Allocate the parts. Have several guards and high priests so every child is involved. Dress up the children, and explain that they are to mime their parts as you tell the story. Give 'sound effects' to anyone except the women and guards. (If you have many children under six years old, don't attempt to allocate roles. It's hard for under-sixes to remember which role they are meant to be playing! The drama will work better if you let everyone act out everything together.)

Tell the story: After Jesus had died on Friday, all his friends were very sad and scared. Very early on Sunday, two women both called Mary came to the tomb where Jesus had been put, carrying special perfume. (*Women tiptoe towards the 'garden'.*) They knew Jesus well and were feeling very sad and frightened. (*Scared faces.*) Soldiers were outside the tomb on guard. (*Guards stand up straight.*)

'How will we move that stone in front of the tomb?' Mary asked as they walked into the garden.

'I don't know,' said the other Mary, 'but we'll find a way, maybe someone will help.'

They were almost at the tomb when suddenly there was loud banging and crashing. (*Sound effects.*) It was an earthquake. Everything shook. (*Women and guards shake.*) Then they all saw the angel. He rolled back the stone and sat on it. (*Angel mimes this.*) He looked like lightning and his clothes were white as snow. The soldiers were so afraid that they shook and fell down. (*The guards fall down.*) The women stood rigid because they were so afraid.

'Don't be afraid,' the angel said. 'I know you are looking for Jesus who died on the cross, but he is not here. He has risen, just as he said he would. Come and see where he lay (*beckons*), then go and tell his disciples that he has risen and has gone ahead of you to Galilee. You will see him there.' (*Exit angel.*)

The women were so excited (*jump for joy*) but also a little afraid. (*Scared faces.*) They hurried away (*Begin to do so.*) and suddenly they met Jesus. (*Enter Jesus.*) They fell at his feet, but Jesus said, 'Don't be afraid. Go and tell my friends to go to Galilee and they will see me there.' (*Jesus points.*)

The women were so excited as they ran to find the disciples. (*Exit Jesus, exit women excitedly.*)

Meanwhile the guards had recovered and went to tell the high priests what had happened. (*Guards get up; high priests come to meet them.*)

'You'll never guess, we were so scared, there was an earthquake and an angel and the stone rolled away and he's gone. Jesus – he's gone, there's nothing in the tomb,' the guards blurted out. (*Guards act agitated.*)

The high priests were very concerned and plotted together. (*Priests look worried and murmur together.*)

'Look here,' the high priests said, 'here's some money. Just say that the disciples stole his body in the night whilst you slept. We'll fix it with the governor, you won't get into trouble. Make sure you keep to this story.' (*Priests give over money bags.*) The guards took the money. (*Exit priests and soldiers.*)

Some people believed the guards, but we know that what the angel told the women is true. Jesus is our risen king! (*Everyone shouts 'hurrah!'*)

I was there

A dramatisation of the Easter story for four readers

All the characters stand in a line and step forward when it is their turn to speak. After they have spoken, they freeze in an appropriate pose until it is their turn to speak again.

Soldier: Well, it was another day's work, but not a nice one. Three people to nail to crosses. Two of them were really bad men, but that man Jesus, he didn't seem to have done anything wrong except to annoy some important people. Even so, people were shouting and making fun of him. Only a little while ago they were asking him to make people well and listening to his stories. Some of his friends were there crying. They must be wondering why this has happened when Jesus seemed such a good man. Yes, it's been a horrible scary sort of day. As well as watching those poor people on the crosses it's been very dark and we've had an earthquake. Still, it's over now and all three are dead. But that Jesus, he was special. I reckon he might have been the Son of God, just as he said.

Mary Magdalene: It's been a horrible day. Jesus, my best friend, has died. Those Roman soldiers nailed him to a wooden cross. It was only a job to them and they had orders to do it, but I hated hearing other people shouting horrid things to Jesus. A group of us stood and watched. I can't imagine life without Jesus. I don't think I will ever stop crying.

Joseph: What a dreadful day! Being rich doesn't make you happy, not when you see a good man dying like Jesus did. But I was glad to be able to help a little. In my garden I've got a new tomb cut into a cave. The Roman governor let me have Jesus' body. His friends and I wrapped it in a clean cloth, put it in the cave and rolled a huge stone over the entrance. So now he's there – dead. I'll never see my friend Jesus again.

Soldier: Well, Jesus' friends put his body in a cave with a great stone over the entrance, but his enemies didn't seem to think that was enough. They said there had been some talk he might come back to life, and they're afraid his friends will pretend he has. Just in case anyone turns up to steal the body, here I am in the garden in the dark, guarding a dead man! Oh, what's that noise? Another earthquake! And a bright flashing light! Ooo-er!

Mary: The other Mary and I have come to the cave early in the morning. We are nearly there, and the ground is shaking. It sounds like another earthquake, but now we can see an angel! He's rolling away that huge stone and sitting on it! The soldiers who've been left on guard have collapsed on the ground. The angel says Jesus isn't dead any more! 'Come and look in the tomb,' he says. 'Now hurry and tell his friends. You'll see him yourself soon!' And here he is! Jesus is here, talking to us! We can touch him! He's alive!

Meetings with Mary

Drama for children, telling the Easter story

The two characters walk on stage, one from either side, and meet each other in the middle.

Mary: Hello Sarah.

Sarah: Morning, Mary. You look sad.

Mary: Haven't you heard the dreadful news?

Sarah: What news? I wasn't out at all yesterday. Little Samuel wasn't too well.

Mary: It's Jesus. They crucified him yesterday.

Sarah: Crucified him? Oh no! That's terrible. How could they? He was such a good man.

Mary: The Jewish leaders took him to Pilate and he was sentenced to death. It was awful.

Sarah: You weren't there, were you? I've never seen a crucifixion. And I wouldn't want to - it's so horrible.

Mary: Yes I was there. It was more terrible than you could imagine. Our precious teacher made to look like a criminal and in so much pain. It was unbearable.

Sarah: I just can't believe it. I was so sure that Jesus was going to save us from the Romans.

Mary: Yes, I know. How can such a good life come to such a terrible end? There's just no hope now. *(Mary and Sarah walk off.)*

The next day. Mary and Sarah start at opposite sides of room.

Mary: Hey! Sarah! Have you heard the news?

Sarah: What news? How can you be so happy? I thought you cared.

Mary: I do. But Sarah, haven't you heard?

Sarah: Heard what? How can you be so excited when Jesus is dead?

Mary: But that's just it. Jesus isn't dead. At least I don't think he is.

Sarah: What do you mean? I thought you said you saw it happen?

Mary: I did. He was definitely dead. I even saw where they buried him in Joseph's tomb. They put him there on Friday night and I watched them roll a big stone across the entrance.

Sarah: What are you talking about?

Mary: Well, we went to the tomb this morning to put spices on the body. We were trying to work out how we would move the stone, but when we got there, the stone had been moved!

Sarah: Really? Who did it?

Mary: I don't know. But that's not the amazing bit. The tomb was empty!

Sarah: You mean someone had taken the body away?

Mary: No. There was a man there - he looked like an angel. He said, 'Don't be alarmed! You are looking for Jesus from Nazareth. God has raised him to life. He isn't here. Go and tell his disciples that he will go ahead of you to Galilee. You will see him there.'

Sarah: So you think he's alive?

Mary: Well, yes, I think he must be. Don't you remember Jesus said something about being raised to life? Don't tell anyone just now. We could be in real danger if the Jewish leaders find out. I'm really confused. I'm so excited, but I'm also frightened. I have to go and tell the disciples. Do you want to come with me?

Angel story

An Easter Day drama suitable for all ages

Two angels are sitting outside the tomb.

Angel 1: What an amazing day!

Angel 2: It certainly was – incredible!

Angel 1: The most remarkable victory of all time!

Angel 2: Yes, victory over death itself! Surely those humans must understand it now!

Angel 1: Yes – it's amazing how slow they are to grasp the point, isn't it?

Angel 2: That's right – Jesus has spent the last three years with them. He told them that he would die and rise again – but they just didn't get it!

Angel 1: And even now that Mary has seen him alive, they still don't understand.

Angel 2: I felt kind of sorry for Mary as she arrived at the tomb this morning. She wanted to put spices on the body – she was so miserable! I suppose she thought she would be helping God by looking after the body.

Angel 1: Only she didn't realise there was no body to look after!

Angel 2: You'd think that when she saw the body had gone, she would have realised that Jesus was alive, but instead she was even more upset!

Angel 1: Mm. I couldn't understand why she was so upset. That's why I asked her why she was crying.

Angel 2: It was her answer that puzzled me! 'They've taken away my Lord and I don't know where they have put him.' Jesus was alive, but Mary was still looking for a body.

Angel 1: I was just trying to work out how to explain it to her when I saw Jesus approaching, so I thought, 'Great. Jesus is here. Now she'll understand.'

Angel 2: That's what I thought too. But she barely noticed him. She just kept crying.

Angel 1: And did you notice? Jesus asked the same question we did: 'Why are you crying?'

Angel 2: It was kind of funny when you think about it. There she was, desperately looking for Jesus, when he was standing right beside her. She didn't recognise him! I think she must have thought he was the gardener, because she asked him if he'd taken away the body!

Angel 1: I was just wishing she would look into his face and see the love in his eyes – then she would have recognised him.

Angel 2: Yes. But don't you just love the way Jesus always knows the right thing to say or do? All he said was, 'Mary.' That was it, just, 'Mary.'

Angel 1: Then she looked up into his eyes and she knew. What a wonderful sight.

Angel 2: It brought a tear to my eye when she called out, 'Teacher!' What an amazing reunion.

Angel 1: And Jesus gave her just enough time to feel his love and comfort surrounding her, before he sent her off to tell the others the fantastic news.

Angel 2: Isn't Jesus amazing?

Angel 1: He certainly is! I think Mary and the disciples are just beginning to realise how wonderful and powerful and loving and absolutely incredibly fantastic Jesus really is.

Shadow of doubt

A mimed story for Easter-time using shadow play

This mime will work particularly well as a shadow play, acted out between a large white sheet and a bright light (eg OHP) in a darkened room. Check where the mime artists need to stand between the light and the screen to give a good shadow. Switch the light off to create scene changes. Jesus can crouch down so his shadow cannot be seen, and then appear suddenly by standing up at the appropriate time. The narrator should pause at each * while the actors mime the story.

Narrator: Jesus was dead. *(Jesus stands as though nailed to the cross.)* His disciples had watched as the soldiers nailed his hands to the cross * and later stuck a spear in his side. They had seen his body being carried to a tomb* and a large stone rolled across the entrance.*

Now the disciples were afraid. They huddled together in a small room,* behind locked doors.* They were frightened that the Jewish leaders might round them up and crucify them too because they had been followers of Jesus. They were sad because their beloved friend and teacher had died.

Suddenly, Jesus appeared in the middle of the group. *(Jesus appears before the disciples. The disciples are astonished.)* He greeted the disciples and showed them his hands and his side.* The disciples understood that Jesus had come back to life and they were overjoyed. Jesus breathed on them, filling them with the Holy Spirit. He told them to go and tell others about God, just as he had taught them.*

Thomas was one of the twelve disciples but he was not in the room with the others when Jesus appeared. The others told him they had seen the Lord, but Thomas did not believe them. *(Thomas shakes his head in disbelief as another disciple 'tells' him what he saw.)* He had seen Jesus crucified and buried. How could he have come back to life? Thomas said, 'Unless I see the nail scars in his hands and touch them with my finger, and unless I put my hand where the spear went into his side, I will not believe.'*

A week later the disciples were together again and this time Thomas was there too. Jesus came in while the door was still locked* and stood in the middle of the group.

He greeted the disciples, then spoke directly to Thomas. 'Put your finger here and look at my hands! Put your hand in my side.* Stop doubting and have faith!' Thomas was amazed. He knew it was Jesus, and Jesus knew exactly what Thomas had said a week ago. He fell onto his knees in front of Jesus, saying, 'My Lord and my God!'*

All freeze.

Paid on the nail

A Good Friday drama by Dave Shailer and Andy Riordan

Two smarmy Pharisees move amongst four groups of people (Judas, soldiers, the poor, friends of Barabbas) on stage, giving each a bag of money. Each group exits when they have been paid.

1: Judas, listen to our proposition!

2: We're in a difficult position.

1: We want to get Jesus out of our way.

2: So here's the money, now do what we say.

Judas: What shall I do?

1: Kiss him.

2: Goodbye.

Judas: Paid on the nail.

1: Soldiers, listen to our proposition!

2: We're in a difficult position.

1: We want to get Jesus out of our way.

2: So here's the money, now do what we say.

Soldiers: What shall we do?

1: The man who is kissed.

2: Is the man to arrest.

1: Just bring him here.

2: We'll do the rest.

Soldiers: Paid on the nail.

1: Poor people, listen to our proposition!

2: We're in a difficult position

1: We want to get Jesus out of our way.

2: So here's the money, now do what we say?

Poor: What shall we do?

1: There's going to be a trial.

2: With judges.

1: And juries.

2: And Jesus.

1: And you.

2: They'll listen to what you say.

1: Make sure he won't get away.

2: By lying about him.

1: And about what he said.

2: Make sure he'll end up dead.

Poor: Paid on the nail.

1: Friends of Barabbas, listen to our proposition!

2: We're in a difficult position.

1: We want to get Jesus out of our way.

2: So here's the money, now do what we say.

Friends of Barabbas: What shall we do?

1: We want you to.

2: Shout!

1: Scream!

2: Rant!

1: Rave!

2: When it comes to the choice.

1: It's your friend you must save.

2: Use all your breath.

1: To send Christ to his death.

2: Shout for Barabbas!

1: Get everyone to shout it aloud.

2: So if anyone shouts 'Jesus'.

1: He's lost in the crowd.

2: Barabbas!

1: Barabbas!!

2: Barabbas!!!

1: Barabbas must live!

2: And Jesus must die!

Friends: Paid on the nail.

1: Jesus said he'd die to save men.

2: He'll die all right.

1: He said he would pay for our sin.

2: But instead he'll pay for all the things he said about us.

1: He'll pay for a lot of things.

2: Up there on the cross.

1 and 2: He'll pay on the nail!

A bug's (after) life

An allegory on the theme of resurrection and new life by D Shailer and M Titley

Two people wriggle/inch/crawl onto stage (wearing green sleeping-bags and deely boppers). One eats a piece of lettuce. They stand when they meet each other.

1: My feet are killing me.

2: What? All hundred of them?

1: Yeah, it's no fun being a caterpillar, I can tell you.

2: You don't have to tell me. I only get to play the second half of any football match.

1: Why's that then?

2: Cos I spend the first half putting my boots on.

1: Life's so hard. And all you get to eat is cabbage all day.

2: I'll just call you a melancholy flower then.

1: If only there was more to life than this.

2: Funny you should say that. I've heard... that there is!

1: What? More to life than just trudging around in this hand to mouth, or should I say, foot to mouth existence?

2: I've heard... we can fly.

1: Fly?! You're pulling my legs.

2: No, God's truth. We can fly. Think of it. Freedom. A new perspective on the world. Up there. In the clouds.

1: Did you get out of the wrong side of the flowerbed this morning?

2: No. I just feel we need to turn over a new leaf.

1: Fly? I've never heard such compost.

2: And what's really great is that you've got the potential even now.

1: I... I can't believe it. Look at me: I'm green, I'm fat, I'm ugly...

2: Nonsense. You're not all that green.

1: So how on earth can I fly?

2: We'll be given new bodies and wings.

1: I'm sorry but I just can't imagine it.

2: I don't suppose I can really imagine it either. It'll be totally different. But... but the reason we can't imagine it is because we'll all be transformed.

1: Transformed?

2: Yeah. We won't be big and fat and ugly.

1: And green.

2: We'll be beautiful with bright painted colours.

1: Next, you'll be telling me we'll be light and graceful.

2: Of course. It is beyond what we can imagine. But that doesn't make it impossible. Currently we're earthbound but then...

1: It does sound better than vegetating here.

2: That's right. Who wants to be a has-been...

1: When you could be a will-be?

2: It's what we were created for.

1: All right, all right, all right. So how do you start then?

2: Oh, that's easy. The secret is: you have to be born again.

Freeze.

Stories for children

Stories to help Easter come to life!

One special day

A story for Palm Sunday, based on Luke 19:28–40

You will need: the illustration on page 33

Before you begin, fold the page to show only Jesus and his disciples.

Storyteller: It was daytime. The sun shone brightly as Jesus and his disciples walked to Jerusalem. Sometimes they sang as they walked, and other people joined in. Children skipped happily now that they saw the big city of Jerusalem ahead of them.

Only Jesus was quiet as he walked along. He was looking towards Jerusalem too. He called two of his friends. 'Go ahead,' he said. 'You'll find a young donkey which has never given anyone a ride. Bring it to me.'

Jesus stopped to wait. All the people stopped too, wondering what was going to happen. It was so quiet now that they could hear the wind blowing through the trees. They whispered, 'What's going to happen? Is Jesus going to show us that he's our king?'

Soon they heard the clip-clop of the donkey's hooves on the road. *(Show the picture of the donkey.)* The two friends brought the donkey to Jesus. They took off their coats and put them on the donkey's back. Then they helped Jesus to climb on.

(Show the picture of the crowd waving.) People in the crowd took off their coats too and laid them all along the road into Jerusalem. They said, 'This is a wonderful day. Jesus is our king. He's coming to Jerusalem and everything will be good for us again.'

Jesus told the donkey to walk, and the crowd began to cheer and wave. In the bright sunshine, they watched as Jesus rode the donkey along the road and over the people's coats. And everyone began to cheer!

'Hooray!' they cried out loudly. 'Hooray! Here comes our king, riding on a donkey!'

Even the trees seemed to be waving as the wind blew through their branches. And all the way into Jerusalem the crowd cheered and waved.

Only Jesus was quiet. He looked ahead at the city of Jerusalem. He knew that it was time for him to do something very hard, something that God wanted him to do. It was daytime and the sun shone brightly, but soon it would be night.

The donkey's story

The Palm Sunday story with a home-made puppet

You will need: a donkey puppet made by pasting the picture of the donkey (see page 32) on to a box covered in plain paper.

Introduce the donkey and explain that he is going to tell the story:

Storyteller: Hello everyone, do you know what kind of animal I am? Yes, I'm a donkey. Can you bray like a donkey? Wonderful! What lovely singing! I'm going to tell you about the most exciting day I've ever had. Listen...

Long ago, when I was very young, before I'd even given a single ride on my back, my mother and I were standing together enjoying the spring sunshine when two men came and untied us.

Hey!' shouted our owner. 'What do you think you're doing?'

The two men told him that Jesus needed us and he would send us back quite soon. Our owner said, 'Well, that's fine, of course.' So, off we went, down the dusty road. *(The children could make clip-clop sounds with their tongues.)*

Jesus was waiting for us. I had never seen him before, but I felt so excited. He seemed very special, like a king. The two men put their coats over my back and Jesus climbed on. You know, I wasn't scared. I was just so happy and proud to carry him.

There were people everywhere – in front of us, behind us and next to us, all waving, laughing and dancing. They shouted 'Hosanna! Hosanna to Jesus, the king!'

That wasn't all, though. People made a lovely carpet for us to walk on, throwing down their coats on to the road and cutting down branches from the trees. I knew that I must be carrying a most important king. I'll never ever forget that day.

Cut

Fold

Fold

Cut

One special night

The story of the Last Supper, based on Luke 22:1–23

You will need: the illustration on page 33

Before you begin, fold the page to show only Jesus and his friends.

Storyteller: It was night-time. As Jesus and his friends walked through the streets of Jerusalem, everything was silent. The only noise was their own footsteps.

Peter said quietly, 'When John and I came this way this morning, the streets were full of people. It was so noisy – people shouting, talking and laughing.'

'And,' added John, 'donkeys braying and sheep bleating!' He pointed ahead to some steep steps. 'The room we got ready is up those steps. It was just as you said, Jesus. We saw a man carrying a big jug of water and we followed him to the room upstairs and got the meal ready there.'

It was dark, but John knew the way. *(Show the picture of the room.)* The lights were burning in the room and the meal was laid out on the table. Everyone sat down and looked at Jesus.

He smiled. 'I've been looking forward to sharing this meal with you,' he said. 'In a little while, I have to do something very hard, something that God wants me to do. I will have to leave you for a while.'

Outside it was dark and quiet. Even though the lights were burning inside, everyone felt sad. They didn't want Jesus to go away.

(Show the picture of the bread and wine.) Jesus took a piece of bread and broke it. 'Look,' he said gently, 'my body will be broken just as I've broken the bread. When you eat broken bread, it will help you remember me.' He handed everyone a piece of bread and they ate it.

Then Jesus took a cup of wine. 'This wine is red like my blood,' he explained. 'When you drink it together, it will help you remember me. You will be glad because I am doing something very hard that God wants me to do. I will bleed and die, but I am doing it because I love you.'

Jesus' friends all drank some wine. They were very sad.

But they didn't know that they wouldn't be sad for long. Jesus would die, but he would come back, alive and joyful. Next time they ate broken bread and drank wine together, it would be a happy meal because Jesus would be alive for ever!

The missing piece

The story of Jesus' arrest and trial using a jigsaw puzzle

You will need: the illustration on page 35 enlarged onto card and cut into sections

Have the puzzle pieces one to six ready and tell the story using the guide below and the Bible passage. Display the pieces at the right time.

Storyteller

1 It was late at night. Jesus and his friends had had supper together. Jesus talked about the sad things that were going to happen to him. They promised they would not leave him on his own (Matthew 26:31–35).

2 Jesus and his friends went to a garden. Jesus wanted to pray and asked some of them to keep watch with him, but they fell asleep (26:36–46).

3 Judas had left the group earlier. Now he came to the garden with some soldiers. He told them which one was Jesus, and they arrested him, but Jesus did not struggle or fight. As he was taken away, his friends left him and ran away (26:47–56).

4 Jesus was taken to the high priest's house. He was questioned and hit. People told lies about him, but he didn't defend himself (26:57–68).

5 Then Jesus was taken to Pilate, the Roman governor. Pilate didn't think Jesus had done anything wrong, but because everyone was shouting 'nail him to a cross', Pilate agreed this should be done (27:1–26).

6 The soldiers took Jesus back to their fortress and made fun of him. They dressed him up and beat him and spat on him. Then they led him out to be nailed to a cross (27:27–30).

Conclude by saying that although the story does get even sadder when Jesus dies on the cross, we know that there is a happy ending. Hand out piece seven to complete the jigsaw puzzle. This piece shows the wonderful ending which is the Easter Day story.

Jesus feels sad

A story about the arrest of Jesus, based on Matthew 26:36-56

Start by singing 'If you're happy and you know it', using an appropriate tone of voice and body language. Encourage the children to join in with actions and expressions.

'If you're happy and you know it, clap your hands...'
'If you're angry and you know it, stomp your feet...'
'If you're sad and you know it, look unhappy...'
'If you're sleepy and you know it, give a yawn...'

Say that all of us sometimes feel happy, or sad, or angry, or sleepy – and all sorts of other feelings. Explain that Jesus sometimes felt happy or sad, as we do. Explain that you are going to tell the story as though you are one of Jesus' friends who lived long ago.

Storyteller: Hello. My name is Peter. I have a very special best friend. His name is Jesus. I loved to go everywhere with Jesus, listening to what he told people. Sometimes, Jesus was very happy. He loved to sing and to talk to people about God. Sometimes – not very often – I saw Jesus look very cross! And sometimes, Jesus looked sad.

One day we came to a big town called Jerusalem. Everyone was very happy to see Jesus and he looked happy too.

We had a big supper together. We all felt very sleepy. But Jesus looked sad. Jesus said, 'Please don't go to sleep. Wait for me. I want to pray.'

I loved Jesus very much. He was my best friend. And I wanted to wait for him. But I felt so tired that I started to fall asleep. Jesus found me and his other friends sleeping. He woke us up.

'Please wait for me,' he asked. 'Please pray with me.' He looked so sad. I think he had been crying.

I thought, 'I must stay awake. That's what Jesus wants me to do.'

Jesus started praying again. But you know what? I fell asleep again! I felt so tired. Jesus woke us up again. 'Get up,' he said. 'Some people are coming. They want to take me away.'

We got up quickly. Some men came with big swords and they took Jesus away. I felt very sad. I loved Jesus and they took him away to die on the cross.

That is not the end of the story. They did kill Jesus on the cross. That was a bad thing to do and it made me feel very sad. But God made Jesus come alive again. Now I am happy because I know that Jesus is alive!

View from the hill

A monologue for children based on the crucifixion story

You will need: simple Roman-soldier costume (optional)

Ask your listeners to imagine that they are all sitting on a hill near Jerusalem, hearing the story of what happened to a soldier:

Storyteller: I enjoy being a guard. Most of the time I simply stand near the doors to Pilate's rooms, making sure that only the right people get in to see him. It's not hard work, but it's not that exciting either.

But that all changed last Friday when the Captain said, 'We need extra guards at Golgotha today – that religious troublemaker, Jesus, is going to be crucified. We don't want any riots!'

I'd seen Jesus go in to meet Pilate, and he looked tired, weak and harmless. He didn't appear to have done anything wrong, yet they were going to kill him.

Well, it's not my job to ask questions, just to obey orders! So I went to the top of the hill and waited while Jesus and the two criminals were nailed to their crosses. A few of Jesus' friends and family huddled at the foot of his cross, singing, praying and crying. Some priests came along and shouted insults.

By lunchtime, the sky was black and there was a strange feeling in the air, until, at about three, Jesus shouted something and died. Well, it's hard to describe what happened next! It was like a giant had picked up the world and shaken it! People reported strange happenings in the temple and all over town. Afterwards, one of my mates whispered to me 'He must have been the Son of God!', and I had to agree.

I was supposed to have the weekend off, but the next day I heard that the priests were worried about people stealing Jesus' body from his tomb, so I was sent to guard the tomb. There was no way any of Jesus' weak and bedraggled friends could have moved the massive stone we put in front of the tomb, but we had to keep an eye out anyway.

Early on Sunday there was another earthquake which rolled the stone from the tomb door. I saw something really bright, and that's all I remember. I think I must have passed out with the shock. When we reported back to our Captain, he gave us some money and told us to keep our mouths shut about it.

Don't tell anyone what I've told you, will you?

Uncover the truth

The resurrection story combined with 'Pass the parcel'

You will need: the sentences below written out and wrapped in a parcel in reverse order, a dice, small chocolate eggs (optional) in the centre of the parcel.

Give one child the parcel and dice. If they roll a one or six, they undo a layer and read out the sentence. Otherwise, the parcel and dice are passed on. To make the story more dynamic, elaborate a little on each sentence after it has been read out:

1 Jesus died on the cross on Friday.
2 A man called Joseph asked for permission to bury Jesus.
3 Joseph took Jesus' body and wrapped it in clean sheets.
4 Joseph placed the body in a new tomb, dug from solid rock.
5 The women who had followed Jesus saw Joseph sealing the tomb with a large stone.
6 Early on Sunday morning the women came back to the tomb.
7 The women found that the stone had been rolled away.
8 The women were very puzzled, as the body of Jesus was not in the tomb.
9 Two angels appeared, and the women bowed in fear.
10 The angels said, 'Why are you looking here for Jesus? He is not here, he is risen.'
11 The women ran to tell the rest of Jesus' followers.

12 Peter ran to the tomb and found it just as the women had said. He was amazed!

Jesus explains

Jesus' appearance on the Emmaus road, as told by Cleopas

The story could be told by someone dressed as Cleopas, or using a puppet. Introduce 'Cleopas', explaining that he was not one of Jesus' twelve special friends (disciples), but another person who had been a friend of Jesus. Continue as follows:

Storyteller: Hello, my name is Cleopas and I live in Emmaus. That's a village about seven miles away from the capital city of Jerusalem. I'm going to tell you about something very exciting which happened to me a short time ago. Have you heard about Jesus? Well, I was one of his followers. When he came up to Jerusalem, I spent many hours listening to his teaching. His messages from God were wonderful and I was amazed at the things he did and the way he cared for people. But then, of course, he was nailed on the cross and he died. I *had* thought that he was the Messiah, God's special messenger, but now everything seemed to be over. So my friend and I decided we had better go back home to Emmaus. We felt really sad, and on the way we talked about everything that had happened to Jesus.

Then someone else came up and started walking with us. It is quite usual for people to walk together along country roads, as it is safer to be in groups than on your own. He asked what we were talking about. We were really surprised that he didn't know what had been going on in Jerusalem, so we explained all about Jesus and how he had been put to death on the cross. Not only were we feeling sad, but very puzzled too, as we had heard rumours that Jesus was alive. Some of the women had even said that they'd seen him! We knew that it couldn't possibly be true, and so we were really confused.

Then the man started to explain everything to us. He reminded us of things written in the Scriptures long ago by Moses and all the other prophets, that showed us that the Messiah would have to die and would then be raised to life again. Gradually we began to understand that what had happened showed that Jesus really was the Messiah and that it was all part of God's plan.

By now we had reached our house. As it was getting late we invited the stranger to stay with us. We got supper ready and sat down at the table. We asked our visitor to say thank you to God for us. The man took the bread, gave thanks to God, broke the bread and gave it to us. And then suddenly we recognised him. We realised that the stranger was Jesus! The rumours were true – he really was alive! No wonder he had been able to explain everything so well. Then Jesus disappeared. But we were so excited that we got up from the table and ran all the way back to Jerusalem to tell the good news to the rest of the believers.

Easter garden story

The story from Palm Sunday to Easter Day, combined with making an Easter garden

You will need: roasting pans (foil ones will do) for individual gardens, or a large container such as a dog basket or nursery sand tray for a group garden, a waterproof lining if necessary, compost, stones, including one large flat one, moss (or possibly turf for a very large garden), a tin or cup, grey or brown plasticine or clay, straight twigs or flat craft sticks, string, glue or chenille wires, small jars or bottle tops, evergreen hedge trimmings (optional), small plants or 'trees', a small piece of white cloth, small flowers (real or artificial)

The story: Tell the Easter story as you build up and rearrange an Easter garden. Chat with the group as you do so, encouraging them to talk about the parts of the story that they know. Pause at each section as you read the story from the Bible. The passages given here are suggestions only. You may want to omit the Palm Sunday story and just talk about Good Friday and Easter Sunday.

First, with the children, build the structure of your garden. Put a layer of compost across the bottom, then lie the cup on its side in one far corner with the opening facing inwards, to make the tomb. Make a platform inside the tomb with plasticine or clay. Build a hillside over the tomb with more compost, pressing it down firmly. Lay a stone pathway leading to the tomb, then cover the remaining compost with moss. Keep the large flat stone to one side, but arrange any others decoratively in the garden. Also arrange the small jars/bottle tops wherever you will want flowers later, and plant any small plants and 'trees'. Make sure you keep the top of the hill clear. Say to the children that you are going to tell the story about Jesus. It is a story that we can read in the Bible.

Storyteller: Jesus was a very good man. The Bible tells us of many amazing things that he did, like making sick people well and blind people see. Once, 5,000 people came to listen to him, and he fed them all with just a small amount of food. *(Ask the children if they can tell you any of the wonderful things that Jesus did.)* But Jesus didn't only do miraculous things. He also made friends with people – people who were bad and who others didn't like – and they changed into happy, good people. He welcomed strangers, foreigners and children, rich and poor people. He talked about God in a way that people understood, and he helped them to know God too. In all the stories about Jesus in the Bible, there isn't one which says he ever did anything bad. He was a truly good man.

So it's not surprising that when Jesus rode into Jerusalem on a donkey, the people began to cheer. To them Jesus seemed like a king, and here he was, riding into their capital city. They put branches from palm trees on the road like a carpet and shouted out loudly that their king was coming! *(Let the children lay the evergreen clippings along the path. Read the story from Mark 11:7–10.)*

But not everyone liked Jesus. Some of the leaders were jealous of him. Some thought he was going to change the way people had behaved for hundreds of years. They did not mind that God did not like the way people were behaving, and they did not realise that Jesus' way was what God wanted. The Romans who had conquered the country were not happy about Jesus either. A leader who got all the people on his side could be dangerous. They watched Jesus carefully.

Stories for children

In the end it was one of Jesus' own friends who betrayed him. He told the leaders when Jesus would be in a quiet place with just a few friends, and they came with a big group of soldiers and they took him away. Amazingly, Jesus didn't struggle or try to run away. He was frightened and sad, but somehow he knew that what was happening to him was what God wanted.

Lies were told about Jesus, and an excuse was made to put him to death. The Roman soldiers led him out of Jerusalem, along with two other men who were criminals. They carried heavy wooden crosses to the top of the hill. *(Let the children make three crosses from the twigs of flat sticks, fixing them with glue, string or chenille wires. Push them into the compost on top of the hill. Listen to what happened.) Read the story from Luke 23:32-35, 44-46.)*

One of Jesus' friends was a rich man called Joseph. Like the others he was very sad, but he thought of one last thing he could do for his friend Jesus. He and a few others had to work quite quickly, as it was getting dark. Tomorrow, Saturday, was their special Sabbath day when no one was allowed to work. Listen to what he did. *(Read Luke 23:52-54. Fold the white cloth carefully and put it in the tomb.)*

Some women who were watching, wished there was time to make the tomb nice for Jesus. They decided to come back as soon as they could on Sunday, bringing some sweet-smelling spices. The last thing they saw before they went home was the men rolling a huge stone in front of the tomb to act as a door. They were very sad because they had lost their best friend. *(Place the large stone in front of the tomb.)*

Saturday was a very sad day for Jesus' friends. They must have puzzled and puzzled over why such a good man had been put to death. But on Sunday, something happened to change everything. The group of women got up very early. Let's hear what happened. *(Read Mark 16:1-4. Take away the stone from the entrance of the tomb. Read verses 5 and 6.)*

It was true! Jesus wasn't dead any longer and later that day, and on the days following, many of his friends saw him, talked with him and even ate with him. Forty days later they saw him go back to heaven, but they still carried on talking to him, as his friends do today. *(Decorate the garden with the flowers as a symbol of joy that Jesus came alive again, and remind the children*

again of how the garden tells the whole story – Jesus riding to Jerusalem, Jesus dying on a cross, and Jesus coming to life again.)

But what about that puzzling question of why it all happened? Long, long ago near the beginning of time, in another garden, people had started to disobey God, and they had gone on doing bad things ever since. No one had ever been completely good, and only the completely good could live in the perfect place that God had prepared for the end of time. So God came himself as a man, Jesus, who was completely good. When he died, it wasn't because he was bad but on behalf of all the people in the world, including us, who have ever done bad things. And to prove that God will now accept us as completely good if we ask him to, Jesus came alive again.

Mary meditation

A story for young people and adults, suitable for Easter Sunday

Ask everyone to be still, trying to get into the thoughts and feelings of the person who is about to speak. Then read the following:

Storyteller: You feel restless. You haven't slept for three days. Your eyes are red and swollen from your tears. Outside, it is still dark, but you cannot wait any longer. You must go to him. You collect the ointments and spices you will use to anoint his body, and slip quietly out of the house. The sun is beginning to rise, but the ground is still wet with dew. You hurry through the streets of the city – you can still feel the tension and fear of Friday. You hurry faster.

As you reach the outskirts, you slow a little. You begin to think about the task ahead. It is not a pleasant task. It is one you never imagined you would be doing. You thought he could never die. Your master. Your Lord. He was the centre of your life. Nothing made sense without him. Nothing makes sense now that he is gone.

You remember the day you first met him. When he saw your suffering; he saw you, amongst all those people, and he healed you with one touch of his hand. Years of pain and torment gone – in an instant. Your mind and body free and whole once more. All you wanted to do was worship this man, Jesus. To love him and serve him and, somehow, show him how thankful you were.

So you joined his group of followers. You travelled with him; you prepared food for him; you found places for him to rest. And you listened as he taught the crowds and shared his wisdom with his closest friends. You saw him heal so many people, just as he had healed you. You watched, anxiously, as his enemies grew more hostile. But you believed in his power to overcome them. You believed he was the promised Messiah.

But what do you believe now? He is dead. You watched him die. You stood and watched as hard nails were hammered through his flesh and his body was hauled brutally onto the cross. You watched as he struggled to breathe; you saw the pain in his face as each breath grew weaker. You saw the despair in his eyes. You heard him cry out to God, and then you watched him die.

You still can't quite believe that he is really gone. You reach the tomb, where you saw him taken on Friday, and the stone rolled across the entrance. But you stop, stunned. The stone has been rolled away! What does this mean? You are suddenly afraid. You cannot go in. You turn and run.

You run back to find Peter. He will know what to do. Breathlessly you tell him what you saw. He sets off straight away, running to the tomb. Another disciple goes too. You try to follow, but you can't keep up. Tears are streaming down your face. What can it mean? Where is Jesus?

You reach the tomb just as the two disciples are coming out. They tell you it is empty. There is no body. They leave, scared and confused. But you stay. You have to see for yourself. You look into the tomb and are dazzled by a bright light. You blink away the tears from your eyes. Two angels, dressed in white, are sitting in the tomb. 'Why are you crying?' they ask. You tell them why. You tell them Jesus is gone.

But then you hear a noise behind you. You turn and see a man standing outside the tomb. He asks you, 'Why are you crying? Who are you looking for?' You are terrified, but desperate to understand. You think, perhaps this man is the gardener and has moved the body. You ask him where he has put it.

The man says your name. He knows your name. And you recognise the voice. It is the voice of the one you love. Your Lord. It is Jesus!

Stories for young people

Just the facts

A story activity for 11 to 14s

Jesus was travelling towards Jerusalem. Near the Mount of Olives, Jesus sent two of his disciples on ahead to the next village to collect an unridden donkey. He said that if they were questioned about the donkey, they should just say that the Lord needed it. Everything happened just as Jesus said, and the donkey arrived with the two disciples.

Jesus rode on the donkey, and the crowd cheered and praised God. They shouted, 'Blessed is the King who comes in the name of the Lord!' But some of the Pharisees were not happy.

Jesus arrived in Jerusalem and began teaching in the Temple. The chief priests, teachers of the Law of Moses and others did not like Jesus' teaching, nor the fact that he was popular with the people. Judas, one of Jesus' disciples, arranged to betray Jesus to the leaders who were against him.

The Passover time was near. Jesus ate the Passover meal with his disciples, sharing bread and wine with them as a symbol of his body and blood.

While they were eating, Jesus said that one of his friends would betray him. He went out to pray, but the disciples who were with him fell asleep. A crowd arrived, and Judas came up and kissed Jesus. This was the sign the guards were waiting for, they knew Jesus was the one they had to arrest. Jesus made no attempt to struggle, and was led away.

He was brought before the Jewish council and questioned, then he was taken to see Pontius Pilate, the Roman Governor. Pilate also asked him questions, then when he found out where Jesus was from, he sent him to King Herod, the ruler of Galilee. He too asked questions. Soldiers made fun of Jesus. Herod sent Jesus back to Pilate, who said he could not find Jesus guilty of any crime. But he did not want to upset the Jewish leaders, so Pilate decided to ask the crowd of people what he should do with Jesus. Should he be released? The crowd asked for Barabbas, a known criminal, to be released instead of Jesus. They shouted for Jesus to be crucified.

Pilate gave in to the crowd. Jesus was given a cross to carry. He was badly injured from being beaten and couldn't carry it, so some of the soldiers made a man called Simon, from Cyrene, carry the cross instead.

Jesus was taken to a place called 'The Skull'. He was nailed to the cross, and two criminals were crucified with him. Jesus prayed for forgiveness for those who crucified him.

Around midday, the sky turned dark, and the sun stopped shining. Jesus prayed to his heavenly Father and died.

Joseph of Arimathea asked to bury Jesus' body. He was buried in a tomb in a rock, and a large stone was rolled in front of the tomb.

When you have read the story to the young people, comment on two things. Say that the story is very basic, there are very few adjectives to describe what went on, and there isn't much emotion in the story. Ask the young people to think about what emotions they might be feeling at different times in the story and also how they would describe the events.

Say also that the story stops before it should – that there is still more to say. In twos or threes, ask the young people to finish the story off, using lots of description and thinking about the emotions the characters in the narrative would have been experiencing.

Easter frieze

Daytime and night-time pictures for younger children to make

You will need: green, yellow and grey paint, brushes, large background paper, adhesive, coloured paper cut to shape (see below); dried green herbs; gold or silver stars; protective and clean-up equipment, kitchen roll

Palm Sunday picture

Colour-wash a large piece of paper with watery paints of green and yellow. If this does not dry quickly, dab with pieces of kitchen roll. Create palm trees by pasting on brown paper trunks and add pre-cut leaves at the top. Spread adhesive over the lower two-thirds of the picture and scatter small amounts of dried green herbs over it. Remove loose herbs by carefully shaking the picture outside. Add children's pictures of the crowd and Jesus on a donkey.

Maundy Thursday picture

Colour-wash a large piece of paper with watery grey or black paint. Paste a circle of yellow paper in the centre and on top, children's pictures of the bread and wine. Paste pre-cut shapes of small, flat-roofed houses in silhouette, with one house (which you will need to position yourself) large enough to have a door which opens to reveal a picture of bread and wine. Cover the top third of the picture with stars.

Get the flags out

Flags and bunting for a Palm Sunday celebration

Ask the children to write short praise prayers on pieces of brightly coloured A4 paper (phrases such as 'Hosanna!' or 'King Jesus!' or 'Welcome!' would be appropriate). Secure a green garden stick along one side of each sheet to make a flag – a modern version of a palm branch.

Alternatively, cut out squares of paper, folded in half diagonally. Get the children to write on one or both outer sides of the triangles, then fix them to a length of ribbon or coloured string by 'hanging' them along the fold and securing with staples to make bunting.

Praise scarves

A simple 'make' suitable for Palm Sunday

You will need: lengths of different-coloured crepe paper (75 x 25 cm), one per child; coloured paper, felt-tip pens, crayons, glitter, adhesive sticks, scissors, stapler

Ask the children if they have ever been to a sporting event, or seen one on TV, where the crowds are supporting their team. What do they wave? How do we know which team they support?

Remind the children how excited the people were when they saw King Jesus coming into Jerusalem on Palm Sunday. How could we show Jesus that we want him as our king?

Help the children make 'praise scarves'. Cut a large letter J from coloured paper, explaining that this is the first letter of the name Jesus, and decorate it with felt-tip pens and glitter. Make a fringe on either end of the crepe paper length and then staple the paper 'J' to the centre of the scarf.

Show the children how to hold the scarf above their heads, and wave it from side to side and shout: 'Hip, hip hooray for King Jesus!'

Waving palms

Another easy Palm Sunday craft for children

You will need: newspaper, sticky tape, scissors

Give each child a sheet of newspaper. Help them to roll the paper tightly into a cylinder and fasten the end down with a long length of sticky tape.

They should then cut or tear down strips of paper to half way along the cylinder. Pull the centre upwards gently, twisting slightly to produce a palm-tree shape. These can be waved while singing, dancing and praising God.

Easter craft

Glittery poster

A poster for younger children to celebrate Jesus being alive

You will need: a large piece of card with the outline of the words 'Jesus is alive' written on it (use tall letters about 15 cm high), PVA adhesive, spreaders, glitter, and/or play sand and newspaper

Read the words to the children and let them repeat them with you. Spread some adhesive inside the letter 'J' and then sprinkle glitter and/or sand over it. Repeat this with the other letters, allowing the children to take turns to sprinkle the glitter and sand. If you have a large number of children, you may prefer to have smaller groups, each with a leader. They can then work on a single word or a few letters which can be put together later.

Sprinkle excess glitter and sand on to the newspaper, put the words in order if necessary, and admire the finished result. 'Read' it together once again.

To conclude you could join in this simple praise chant, repeating it loudly several times: Jesus is alive today. Jesus is alive! Hooray!

Easter egg glory

A gift to make for Easter-time

You will need: polystyrene or plastic eggs (available from good craft shops), snips of ribbon, sequins, shiny paper, stars etc, glue sticks, scissors, crumpled newspaper

Gather the children around tables which have been protected with newspaper (or similar) and talk for a while about the Easter eggs they have received. Explain that Easter day is such a wonderful day that people like to give their friends beautiful eggs. Show the plain eggs and ask the children to make them beautiful by pasting the collage bits on. Support the egg in a nest of crumpled newspaper to keep it steady.

Talk together about all the different kinds of eggs there are: eggs to eat, chocolate eggs, decorated eggs, and all the different eggs that living creatures hatch out of: birds, insects, snakes, lizards. Eggs remind us of new life, just as the Easter story does.

When finished, set the eggs to dry.

Son rise painting

An Easter poster for younger children

You will need: large sheet of paper, finger paints in yellows, oranges and reds, protective and clean-up material

Prepare a large sheet of paper with the words 'Jesus is alive today' in the centre. Read the words to the children. Show how to use the finger paints to make lines radiating out from the centre like the rays of the sun. When the picture is finished and hands have been washed, all sit around the picture, admire it, and think of how it reminds us that God is wonderful. Thank and praise God that we can each know Jesus ourselves, because he's alive today.

Group Easter garden

An activity for Easter Sunday (or thereabouts)

You will need: a large deep tray filled with soil or wet sand, small flowers, twigs, leaves, grass, pebbles, a margarine tub or similar for tomb, black tissue paper, glue, pipe cleaners, scraps of material and paper, drawing materials, scissors

Together, arrange the garden with flowers, trees, paths etc, making sure you leave a space for the tomb. Make the tomb by covering the margarine tub with black paper inside and out; put stones in to weight it and put it on its side in the garden and cover the top with grass or twigs so it appears to be in the side of a mound.

Make the people (angel, Jesus, two women and two to four guards) with pipe cleaners. Use two pipe cleaners per person, one to twist to make the head and the legs, the other to be the arms. Dress the figures appropriately as angel, Jesus, guards or women, with scraps of material or paper cut and glued on. Draw paper faces and glue on.

Easter message

An Easter card made from card, paper and chalks

You will need: white and black paper, plain folded cards, coloured chalks and fixing spray, glue, writing materials

Colour a piece of white paper (slightly smaller than the front of the card) with chalk. Start with brown at the bottom and move through red and orange to yellow at the top. Use fingers to merge the colours. An adult should put the fixing spray over the chalk to 'fix' it.

Cut out a cross shape from black paper and glue it on top of the chalk colours. Glue the paper to the front of the card. On the inside right, write in large letters 'Jesus is alive!'

Easter tree

A simple tree with your own Easter message

You will need: twigs, small plastic pots, plasticine, pre-cut card egg shapes, small stickers, felt-tip pens, thread, hole punch

Fill the pots about half full of plasticine. Push a twig into the plasticine so that it stands up straight. On one side of the card egg shapes, write an Easter message, and decorate the other side with stickers or colourful patterns.

Make a hole at the top of each egg, and hang them on the twigs. Allow a generous amount of thread, so that the egg shapes can move round to show both sides.

Rolled away!

Painting stones as a take-home reminder that Jesus is alive

You will need: poster or acrylic paints, brushes, aprons, a large flat stone for each person, the words 'Risen' and/or 'Alive' written out to copy

Remind everyone that the stone was rolled away from the place where Jesus was buried because he was risen. He was alive again. Show them the stones and explain that you are going to decorate them as a reminder that Jesus is still alive.

Everyone should choose a stone and paint one of the words on it, then decorate around the word as they wish, eg with butterflies, flowers, patterns. Do not decorate under the stone or the wet paint on the top will be spoilt.

Fold-up cards

Photocopiable fold-up cards for Easter

You will need: copies of pages 45 and/or 46, art materials such as crayons and felt-tip pens, envelopes (optional)

Give out copies of the fold-up cards from page 45 or 46. Ask the children to think about whom they might give the card to – parents or carers, other relatives, people in church or at school.

Encourage the children to decorate their cards and fold them up so they stand up, with the front of the card showing. If you wish, give the children envelopes to put their cards in.

Small Easter garden

A yogurt-pot garden that will go on growing

You will need: corner-type yogurt pots (where fruit/topping and yoghurt are in separate sections of the pot, the artwork from page 47 copied on to card for each person, sticky tape, sterile compost, fast-growing seeds (eg cress), colouring pens, scissors

Each person colours the background artwork and cuts down the dotted lines carefully. Fold up the corner of the pot and insert it through the cut-out. Tape the card around the main pot. Cut out and stick the card 'stone' across the 'tomb'. Fill the pot with compost and sow the seeds.

Jesus isn't here! He has been raised from death.

Luke 24:6

Happy Easter!
From

Hooray!

Jesus is alive!

This card has been coloured for you by _____

Happy Easter!

From

Happy Easter!

To

Jesus isn't here! God has raised him to life, just as Jesus said he would.

Matthew 28:6

This card has been created
for you by _____

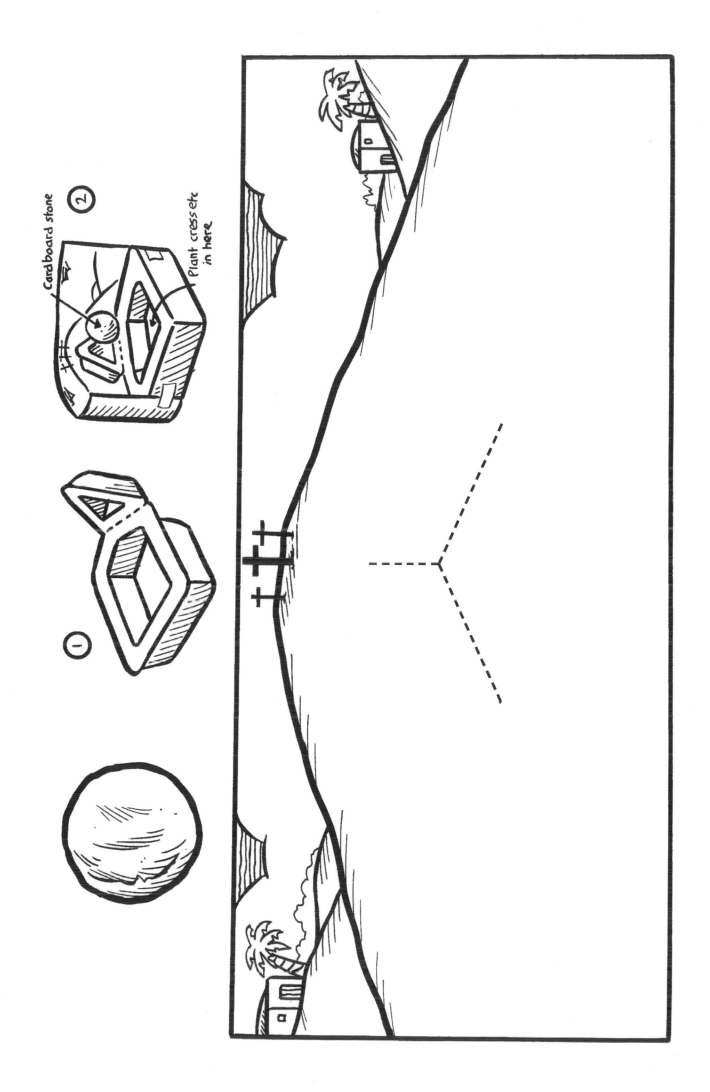

Donkey in a spin

An optical illusion based on the Palm Sunday story

You will need: copies of the picture below, scissors, cocktail sticks, sticky tape, glue, colouring materials

Cut out and colour the pictures, then fold along the dotted line. Tape a cocktail stick to the middle of the back of one of the pictures, as shown in the diagram. Glue the two sides together. Spin the stick between your fingers. Jesus will appear to sit on the donkey when the spinner is spun at the correct speed.

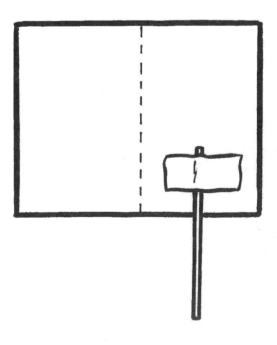

Palm crosses

Making palm crosses from paper

To make a Palm Cross ~

1 Cut off three strips from the long side of a sheet of A4 paper. Each strip should be approximately 15 mm wide. One strip will be used to form the crosspiece. Join together the other two strips with sticky tape and use this longer strip to form the upright of the cross.

2 Make two folds on one end of each strip approximately 15 mm apart.

(Fig.1 folds 1 and 2, Fig.2 folds 3 and 4).

3 Join the two strips together by using the folds already made as a kind of 'hook' on the end of each strip. (Fig.3 folds 5,6,7). You will now have a firm join at this crossover point. Make sure that the loose end of the crosspiece is to the right and the loose end of the longer strip hangs down over the front of the crossover point.

4 Take the loose end of the crosspiece and fold it forward leaving a loop of paper of about 5 cm sticking out to one side.(Fig.4 fold 8). Pass the loose end underneath the long strip hanging down at the front.

5 Form another loop sticking out 5 cm on the other side by folding the loose end of the crosspiece and tucking it into the back of the crossover point. (Fig.4 fold 9 tuck 10). The crosspiece should now stick out evenly about 5 cm either side of the crossover point.

6 The long strip should still be hanging forward over the crossover point. Take the loose end and tuck it upward through the loop at the back of the crossover point, pull the strip right through and a firm knot is formed. (Fig.5 tuck 11).

7 Fold the loose end backward leaving a loop of paper sticking up about 7 cm. to form the top piece of the cross. (Fig.6 fold 12).....

..... Take the loose end and tuck it down the back loop of the crossover point pulling it through until the top loop forms neatly. (Fig.6 tuck 13).

8 Finally, take the loose end of the strip and tuck it into the front of the crossover point leaving a loop of paper hanging down about 14 cm. to form the lower part of the cross. Press at the bottom to form a neat fold. (Fig.7 fold 14 tuck 15).

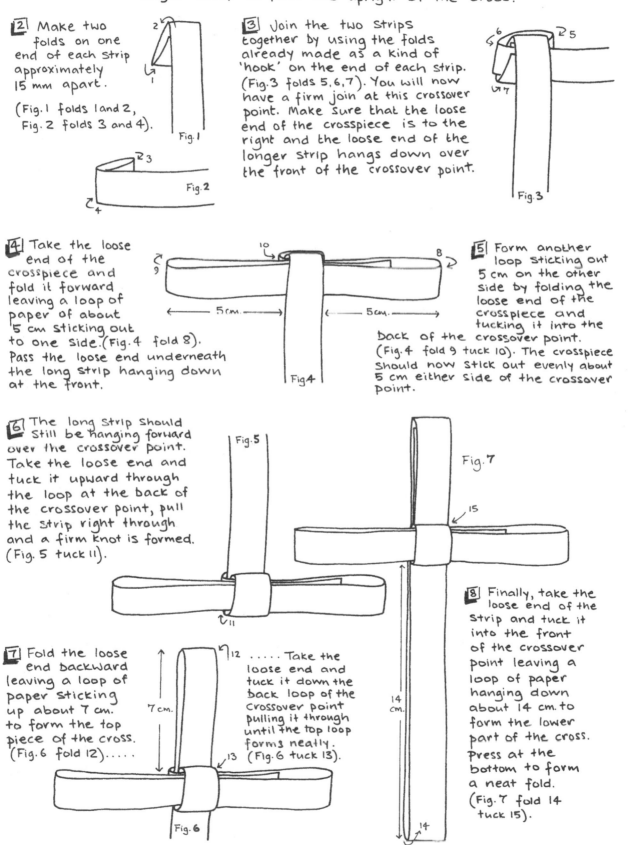

You will need: the template below copied onto stiff card, a finished basket, colouring/writing materials, stapler or sticky tape, shredded tissue paper and mini-eggs

Decorate the four sides of the box and the handle with Easter pictures and phrases praising Jesus, for example, 'Hooray! Jesus is alive'. Fix the sides and handle with staples or sticky tape. Put the tissue paper pieces into the basket and place the mini-eggs on top.

Decorate this handle

Tuck in and stick down.	is	Tuck in and stick down.
Jesus		alive
Tuck in and stick down.		Tuck in and stick down.

Son rise

A stand-up Easter card

You will need: an A5 piece of thin white or green card for each child, a 9 cm diameter circle of white card for each person, glue, colouring materials, scissors, craft knife (adult use only), the diagram below

Give out the A5 card. Colour one side to look like grass. Fold the card in half with the coloured side outside. Then fold each end up to the centre, making four sections (1). Fold the card

into a triangular shape, gluing one end section on top of the other end section (2), to make a prism-shaped hill (3).

Take the card circle, colour it yellow and write 'Son Rise' on it. Using the craft knife, cut a slot in the top fold of the hill just wide enough to slip the sun into (adult only). Complete the card by slipping the sun into the slot (4).

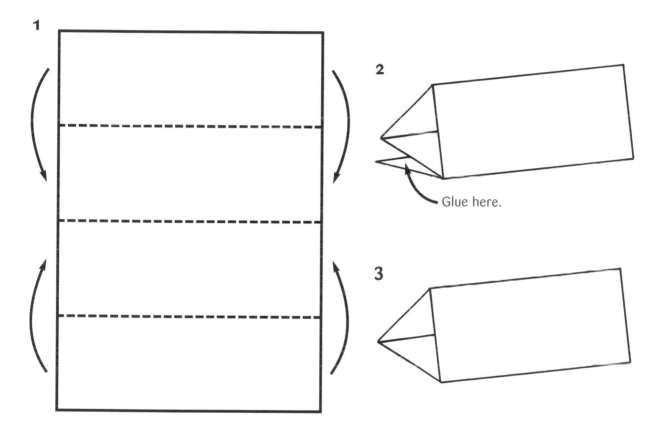

Glue here.

Here comes our King!

A service for Palm Sunday by Christine Wright

You will need: palms, ribbons or streamers; pictures of a donkey (see page 32); outer clothing (to represent disciples); branches or palms (to represent the crowds); labels for display tables saying 'Living to serve others', 'Showing who Jesus is', 'A life of praise'

Procession

Open the service with a procession, either from outside or inside, around the building. Give out palms, ribbons or streamers to wave. Either sing a well-known Palm Sunday hymn or shout 'Hosanna!' as you walk.

Psalm

When everyone is seated, introduce the following verses based on Psalm 24, explaining that in Old Testament times, long before Jesus was born, God's people had a song to sing when they were entering Jerusalem in procession. We can use it today to welcome God into our service.

Sing praise to God who made the world
Sing praise, sing praise to God!
We who live on earth are his.
Sing praise, sing praise to God!

Welcome God, all those who love him.
Welcome him and praise him.
God blesses us when we obey him.
Welcome him and praise him.

Fling wide the gates and welcome him.
Sing praise, sing praise to God!
Open the doors and welcome him.
Sing praise, sing praise to God!

Discussion

Ask the congregation to form small groups where they sit and talk together about their experiences of processions or being in crowds. Allow sufficient time for everyone to have a say, then draw them together again. Gather some of the descriptive words and phrases that have been used and write them up. (The list will be used later in the service.)

Gospel reading

Read Mark 11:1–11. Introduce the reading by saying that it is about what happened on the first Palm Sunday.

Hymn

Throughout the service, choose hymns written for Palm Sunday and others about the kingship and humility of Jesus.

Short talk 1

Who was there on the first Palm Sunday and why?

The donkey
(Show a picture of a donkey.) Jesus needed the donkey to show two things – that he was coming into Jerusalem as a king (Zechariah 9:9) and that he was not coming to make war. He was coming in peace.

The disciples
(Show outer clothing.) The disciples placed their coats on the donkey to make a saddle for Jesus. These close friends of Jesus had been with him since the beginning of his ministry. They'd followed him from the beginning when he was popular with everyone, and through harder times when his enemies had criticised him. Jesus needed his disciples' help (Mark 11:4,7) on his journey into Jerusalem.

The crowds
(Show the branches or palms.) Many people were also on their way into Jerusalem for the Passover festival. When they saw what was happening, they responded by giving Jesus the welcome he deserved (vs 9–10). The words they chanted were, 'God bless him who comes in the name of the Lord!' They may not have understood the full meaning of what Jesus was doing, but they gave him their praise and acclaim. Jesus accepted their praise.

Hymn

Short talk 2

Who is present this Palm Sunday and why? *(During this talk, you will create three 'corners' around the building.)*

Donkeys?
The donkey reminds us of why Jesus came. Our king is someone who comes in peace, to serve others, not to prove his power. When we respond by deciding to live our lives in this way, we are truly his own. *(Each younger child could be given a picture of a donkey to play with and*

Here comes our King!

to keep as a reminder of the Palm Sunday story, but place others on a table with the words 'Living to serve others' on it.)

Disciples?

There *are* disciples in the service – people who are following Jesus day by day through good times and bad. They are ordinary Christians who look much like anyone else, but their words and actions help others to hear and see who Jesus really is. *(Take the outer clothing used earlier and put it on another table which has the words 'Showing who Jesus is' on it.)*

Crowds?

However many people there are in church today, everyone has the chance to catch a glimpse of Jesus and to understand a little more of who he really is. Jesus allowed people to sing his praises: he did not stop them because they didn't have a profound understanding of the suffering he was about to undergo. Today, whether we understand much or little, we can join in the praise of Jesus who comes in the name of the Lord. *(Take the branches or palms used earlier and place them on a third table which has the words 'A life of praise' on it.)*

Prayer of confession and thanksgiving

Humble Jesus, who rode into Jerusalem on a donkey, we confess that we do not always show others the kind of king you really are. Help us to be humble and willing to serve others, just as you were that first Palm Sunday.
We thank you, Lord Jesus, for being our king.

King Jesus, who needed the help of his disciples, we confess that we do not always allow you to speak through our words and actions. Help us to be ready to obey you and let others see who you are and what you can mean to them.
We thank you, Lord Jesus, for being our king.

Generous Lord Jesus, who allowed the crowds to praise him as he rode into Jerusalem, we confess that our praises are sometimes half-hearted. Help us to see as though with new eyes how wonderful you are and how much you have done for us.
We thank you, Lord Jesus, for being our king.

Amen.

Meditation

Invite the congregation to move around the church, stopping at each of the three 'corners' to think about the Palm Sunday story – the donkey, the disciples and the crowds. Suggest that, at each table, they ask themselves what God might want to say to them today. Arrange for quiet music to be playing during this time.

Hymn

Crowd chant

Use the words and phrases collected earlier to create a crowd chant. Give each small group of people a word or phrase and get them to practise chanting it rhythmically. Also practise chanting, as the crowd on Palm Sunday did: 'God bless him who comes in the name of the Lord!' Build the chant as follows: The first group begins chanting its phrase and when it has done so twice, signal for the next group to come in with its phrase and so on. As soon as the last group comes in, the first group should begin to chant 'God bless him who comes in the name of the Lord!' and each group should join them in turn. When everyone is chanting 'God bless him...' signal the congregation to stop.

Blessing

May the King of glory and humility reign in your hearts, giving you courage, joy and hope this Holy Week.

Remember, remember

A Passover meal by Keith Civval

This is a service with a difference – with a meal in the middle of it! Christians can gain new insights into the origins of the communion service; non-Christians can learn about the central basis of the Christian faith in a fresh and informal context; children can be thoroughly involved.

The Jewish festival of Passover goes back to the earliest days, when Israel was formed as God's holy nation. It has been central to the Jewish faith ever since. The Passover teaches us about God's saving purposes in history and this, combined with its informal and interactive character, makes it ideal as a means of presenting the gospel to people of all ages.

Preparation

The meal lies between two times of interactive worship and teaching. It can be an evening meal, or it could be lunch. It can be a family occasion held round the table – or it can be celebrated by a home group, a youth group or other larger grouping. Try to seat everyone round a single table, though for a large group you will need a top table, where the leader sits with the special items and others are seated around other tables so that everyone can see the top table comfortably.

Make as much or as little of the meal as you like, but don't leave it out. It contributes to the sense of informality and it is a good way of drawing everyone into the celebration.

The following food items are essential. They should be set out on each table within easy reach of all the participants.

- Unleavened bread (*matzah*) can be bought in most large supermarkets; alternatively you could use dry water biscuits, which have a similar texture. Alternatively, use the recipe on page 76. You will need a large supply!
- *Charoset* (see page 76) or use the following: chop finely 1 cup of walnuts and 1 green apple; sprinkle with 2 tsp cinnamon and 2 tsp sugar, and stir gently together with wine to the texture of mortar. (This is enough for about eight people.)
- Horseradish, washed and chopped into small pieces but big enough to pick up.
- Sprigs of parsley or any other green herb.
- Bowls of salt water

The leader should have a dish with all of the above *plus* a hard-boiled egg, which has been gently roasted in the oven (till it looks burnt), and a roasted lamb bone. In addition, individually wrap three pieces of *matzah* in a clean napkin and place them in front of the leader. Two candles should be placed on every table.

Prepare a service outline for everyone to follow. In the following outline, normal type indicates words that the leader could use or adapt. Involve as many people as possible, by asking them, in advance, to read selected sections.

Singing is another important feature of Passover. Some songs have been suggested, but you can choose something similar – and if time permits add in more!

The blessing of the wine comes four times during the Passover. It is a good idea to practise this before you start, especially if attempting the Hebrew!

We praise You, O Lord our God, King of the universe, Creator of the fruit of the vine.

Baruch atah adonai, eloheynu melech ha'olam, boreh pori hagafen.

Introduction to the Passover celebration

Words in bold are to be said by all, and words in italics provide general directions or Hebrew transliteration.

Writing about the night before Jesus died, Luke writes: 'When the time came for Jesus and the apostles to eat, he said to them, "I have very much wanted to eat this Passover meal with you before I suffer"' (Luke 22:14). Jesus was going to celebrate in a very similar way to the manner that Jews had celebrated for centuries. We too can look back with thanksgiving on the way God brought the children of Israel out of Egypt, because it was from that nomadic people that God created a nation into which, many generations later, Jesus was to be born.

It is no accident that the climax of Jesus' life on earth came at the Passover season, nor that the final act that Jesus wanted to perform with his disciples, was to celebrate the Passover meal. The apostles were looking back to the time when the people were freed or redeemed from Egypt,

Remember, remember

but Jesus was looking forward to an even greater redemption – the redemption of all mankind from their sin.

The Passover prayer book is called the *Haggadah,* which means storybook, because the Passover is the telling of the story of the escape of the Children of Israel from Egypt – from slavery to freedom. For us today it speaks of the freedom and new life that Jesus has made possible through his death on the cross.

Lighting the candles

We start, as all Jewish festivals start, with the lighting of candles.

It is customary for the woman of the house (or nearest equivalent) to light the candles and say this prayer:

We praise you, O Lord our God, King of the universe, who have blessed us by your commandments and commanded us to kindle the festival lights.

We praise you, O Lord our God, King of the universe. You have chosen us from among all peoples to proclaim your unity throughout the world and to sanctify our lives by obeying your commandments.

In your love, O Lord our God, you have given us holy days for gladness, festivals and sacred seasons for rejoicing, even this Festival of Unleavened Bread, the Season of our Freedom, where we worship you and remember the Exodus from Egypt. For you have chosen us to consecrate us to your service, and given us the festivals for gladness and joy. We praise you, O Lord, who hallow the house of Israel and the festive seasons. Amen.

Opening blessings

There are many customs that accompany the Passover. One is the drinking of four glasses of wine. These are explained as a symbol of freedom because it was the practice of Roman freemen to drink at least four cups of wine and to recline on couches at their banquets. Each glass of wine is preceded with a blessing, which we all say together.

All take a sprig of parsley or cress, dip it in salt water and, before eating it say the following blessing.

We praise you, O Lord our God, King of the universe, who brings forth bread from the earth.

Song: 'Great is the Lord and most worthy of praise'

The leader now takes the middle one of the three matzahs, *breaks it in half, and (later) discreetly hides one piece away somewhere in the room.*

Behold the bread of affliction, which our ancestors ate in the land of Egypt. Let all who are hungry come and eat. Let all who are in want come and celebrate the Passover. This year many are still oppressed; next year may all be free. May this spirit of fellowship fill our hearts, and may the time come soon when no one will be in want, and when a festival of redemption from misery and oppression shall be proclaimed for all mankind. Amen.

The wine glasses are filled, all say the blessing and the first glass of wine is drunk.

Four questions

The *Haggadah* – the dramatic telling of the exodus from Egyptian bondage – is for the entire family. Being child-centred it encourages the children to ask questions concerning the meaning of the service.

The youngest person present asks the following questions:

1 Why is this night different from all other nights? On all other nights we eat leavened or unleavened bread; why tonight only unleavened?

2 On all other nights we eat various herbs; why tonight do we eat bitter herbs?

3 On all other nights we do not dip green herbs in salt water and bitter herbs in *Charoset*; why do we do so tonight?

4 On all other nights we do not have a roasted lamb bone and a roasted egg on the table; why do we have both tonight?

The story of the exodus

We will answer those questions shortly. First we come to the telling of the exodus. We pick up the story at the point at which Moses, having been called by God at the burning bush, had returned to his native Egypt to save the Israelite people. Pharaoh, the king, was not over-keen about letting them go and went through many changes of heart. After each of nine plagues, Pharaoh said that they could go and then changed his mind. And so we come to the final hours in Egypt.

First we have the institution of the Passover celebration: Exodus 12:1–8. The Passover lamb is referred to in the New Testament too. Here is one passage from Peter: read 1 Peter 1:18,19.

Then read the account of the first Passover: Exodus 12:21–39. In your own words, talk about the essential points, using appropriate language. The essential points are: the lamb was without blemish, the lamb was slain, the blood was applied and became the perfect protection from judgement, the people were set free from bondage and having passed through the waters of the Red Sea eventually reached the Promised Land. This is a picture of how Christ, the Lamb of God, was without sin. Just as lambs were slain in Egypt to protect the Israelites, so we too can have new life through Christ's death on the cross.

Song: 'Lord I lift your name on high'

Explanation of the symbols

We have now explained the momentous historical events, which the festival of Passover celebrates. Now we can answer those four questions about how this festival is observed, and especially the symbolic dishes that are before us.

The leader holds up the matzah *and says:*

The first of the Four Questions was about the *matzah*, which is traditionally explained as follows. We eat this *matzah* to remind us of the unleavened bread which our ancestors baked in Egypt because their dough did not have time to ferment before the Almighty revealed himself to them and redeemed them, as it says; 'They left Egypt in such a hurry that they did not have time to prepare any food except the bread dough made without yeast. So they baked it and made thin bread.' (Exodus 12:39).

The leader holds up the horseradish and says:

The second of the Four Questions, about the horseradish, is answered as follows. This horseradish or bitter herb is eaten by us tonight to remind us that the lives of our ancestors were embittered by the Egyptians, as it says 'The Egyptians were cruel to the people of Israel and forced them to make bricks and to mix mortar and to work in the fields.' (Exodus 1:14). For Christians it is a reminder too that the great redemption which God brought on our behalf was a redemption that was brought at great cost.

The leader holds up the charoset *and says:*

The third of the Four Questions was about the dipping of green herbs in salt water, which we have already done, and the horseradish in *charoset* which we shall do presently. The *charoset* was once a common condiment, but as part of the Passover meal it was taken to represent the mortar with which the Israelites were forced to work in Egypt.

The leader holds up the roasted lamb bone and the roasted egg and says:

The last of the Four Questions was about the roasted lamb bone and the roasted egg. The roasted lamb bone is a reminder of the lamb, which was offered as a sacrifice in the temple and then consumed in family groups, together with bitter herbs. The roasted egg is probably a reminder of the burnt offering, offerings which were made on this as on other festivals.

For Jesus at his Last Supper, this was perhaps the most powerful symbol of all. We can recall the fact that his one sacrifice on the cross was made once for all – making all other sacrifices redundant from that time on.

Psalm 113 – read responsively, leader and people reading alternate verses.

Song: 'O Lord my God when I in awesome wonder'

We praise you, O Lord our God, King of the universe, who redeemed us and our ancestors from Egypt, and have enabled us to reach this night, that by eating unleavened bread and bitter herbs we may commemorate our redemption. Cause us, we pray, O Lord our God and God of our fathers, to reach yet other festivals and seasons in peace, heartened in the hope for the

Remember, remember

coming of your kingdom, and rejoicing in the worship of your name. We praise you, O Lord, Redeemer of Israel and all people.

The wine glasses are filled, all say the blessing and the second glass of wine is drunk.

Grace before the meal

The leader breaks and distributes the upper of the three *matzahs* on the dish in front of him and all say:

We praise you, O Lord our God, King of the universe, who brings forth bread from the earth.

The matzah *is eaten. All take a piece of horseradish, dip it* charoset, *and say:*

We praise you, O Lord our God, King of the universe, who has sanctified us by your commandments and commanded us concerning the eating of bitter herbs.

The horseradish is eaten. All take a piece of horseradish between two pieces of matzah. *Then the leader says:*

The Jewish rabbis used to combine *matzah* and horseradish and eat them together so as to fulfil what it says concerning the sacrificial lamb 'Eat the Passover lamb with thin bread and bitter herbs' (Numbers 9:11).

The matzah *and the horseradish are eaten.*

The meal

Use this as an opportunity to talk informally about all that has taken place in the Passover so far. Does it help to explain why the Passover was so important for Jesus?

Conclusion

At the end of the meal ask the children to hunt for the piece of matzah *that was hidden earlier, which the leader then breaks and distributes*

It was the middle piece of *matzah* that was broken, and Jesus said: 'This is my body.' The symbolism is powerful because the breaking earlier represents crucifixion, the hiding signifies burial and now the finding reminds us of Christ's resurrection three days after his death on the cross. We read about it in Matthew 26:26–29.

The wine glasses are filled, all say the blessing and the third glass of wine is drunk.

Song: 'Come and see'

Psalm 115 – *read responsively, leader and people reading alternate verses.*

Psalm 118 – *read responsively, leader and people reading alternate verses.*

The wine glasses are filled, all say the blessing and the fourth glass of wine is drunk.

Psalm 136 – The leader reads the first part of each verse and everyone joins in with the refrain 'His love endures for ever' (NIV).

Song: 'Give thanks to the Lord, our God and King'

Journey's end

A service for Good Friday by Catherine Hammond

This service takes us on a journey through Luke's account of the death of Jesus, divided into sections with congregational response in song or prayer after each. It is a quiet thoughtful service, but also aims to keep the children's interest. There is a very short 'talk', but most of the learning will come through the readings and responses.

Use the material to suit your building, congregation and resources. The aim is to convey Jesus' trial and crucifixion by using movement. For example:

The congregation could move through the church, stopping to listen to readers at different places for different parts of the story - or the readers appear in different places, but the congregation does not move.

Pictures (on OHP transparencies, PowerPoint projection or flip chart) could set the different scenes.

If only one speaking place is available, give each character a very distinctive prop, and get them to walk to this place 'in character'.

Music

Use appropriate music, including hymns and songs, to enhance the content and 'mood' of each section.

Opening hymns
'From heaven you came'; 'Come and see'

During the service
'My Lord what love is this'; 'I'm special'; 'Jesus Christ (once again)'; 'How deep the Father's love for us'; 'The cross has said it all'

Closing hymn
'Oh the mercy of God'; 'There is a redeemer'; 'The head that once was crowned with thorns'

Welcome

Explain the format for this Good Friday service, so that the congregation is put at ease.

Opening prayer

(This could be said together.)
We have come together as the family of God to remember the day that Jesus chose to die for us; to try to understand something of what it must have been like for Jesus to tread the path to the cross, and to wonder at the extent of Jesus' love for us.

Witnesses

Narrator: We shall be following the path Jesus took from very early on the first Good Friday morning until the afternoon of the same day. We shall try to imagine the places he went to, through the eyes of the people who were there. We start at the house of Caiaphas, the chief priest. First we hear from one of the legal experts who was there.

Legal expert: We were summoned to an emergency council meeting in the early hours, so we arrived just before dawn. It was still dark, but the high priest's house was full and buzzing with excitement. We sat in our usual semi-circle for judgement. Then they brought Jesus in. I'd seen him before, teaching in the temple, with people hanging on his every word. Now he was here at our command. He had obviously been beaten. We heard him out, of course, but he was guilty, no doubt of that. Blasphemy would be the charge.

Bible reading
Luke 22:63-71

Song or music

Follow the reading with a song or music.

Witnesses

Narrator: The Jewish council did not have the power to sentence people to death - the death penalty needed to be passed by the Roman governor. In this case it was Pilate. *(Move to Fort Antonia scene.)*

Journey's end

Pilate: My job as Roman governor was to keep peace in this troubled Jewish city. It was important to me to succeed – I did not wish to lose my job. It was Friday, I remember. The Jewish council arrived early, bringing Jesus with them. They said he claimed to be Christ – some sort of king. I couldn't find any basis for the charge. The man was innocent. But they were insistent. To them, blasphemy was a religious offence deserving the death sentence. But this man was not guilty. As he had come from Galilee, I sent him on to Herod, the ruler of Galilee, who happened to be in Jerusalem at the time. *(Move to Herod's palace.)*

Herod: Back in Galilee, I'd heard that Jesus was some sort of miracle-maker, giving blind people their sight, making the disabled dance, even bringing a dead girl back to life. I thought maybe he'd show me a miracle or two – something clever for me to watch. But no, all he did was stand, silent and still. I could have got him released. Stupid of him not to do what I wanted. We made fun of him then – found him a robe fit for a king. It made us laugh – him dressed as a king but with nothing to say.

Song or music

Witnesses

Narrator: So Jesus was taken back to Pilate at Fort Antonia. *(Move.)* Outside, a crowd had gathered.

Crowd member: Yeah, we were there. Me and the family had come up for the feast and we'd stopped to see what was going on. Had to stand on tiptoe, mind, but I saw Pilate, the Roman governor, bring him out. Jesus, he was called, up for claiming to be God. 'Not guilty,' Pilate said. But I'd heard what Jesus had said – the people in front had told me. Someone over to the right started a chant: 'Cru-ci-fy! Cru-ci-fy! Cru-ci-fy!' We joined in. We wanted to see the back of Jesus, and get Barabbas freed.

Bible reading

Luke 23:24,25

Confession

The congregation joins in with the response 'Lord Jesus, please forgive us'.

The religious leaders thought that they were right and closed their minds to God.
We too have made our own minds up and not listened to you.
Lord Jesus, please forgive us.

Pilate knew what was right, but feared for his position and listened to the crowd.
We too have thought more of ourselves than of you.
Lord Jesus, please forgive us.

Herod wanted to meet you for his own amusement.
We too have not made you first in our lives.
Lord Jesus, please forgive us.

The crowd called 'Crucify!' again and again.
We too have often said things that must have hurt you.
Lord Jesus, please forgive us.

Lord Jesus forgive us, save us and help us.
Amen.

Song or music

Witnesses

Narrator: So Pilate handed Jesus over and the soldiers led him away. *(Move to Golgotha.)*

Simon: My name's Simon, and I'm from Libya. I was in Jerusalem at festival time, and saw this group of criminals coming up the track. One of them was stumbling. He couldn't carry the crossbeam. That's why the soldiers told me to pick it up and take it up the hill for him. It wasn't pleasant – the soldiers were shouting insults, and women were crying and wailing. I just did what I was told. The two other prisoners were making a fuss, but Jesus was quiet. He seemed to have a sense of purpose. He was killed at the Place of the Skull.

Bible reading

Luke 23:32-34,44-46

Song or music

All-age talk

(Refer to some of the characters in the story so far, and their reactions to Jesus.) We are not here simply to remember what those people saw and heard, though. We too are involved. Good Friday is for all of us, because it shows us that God's love is vast. It's a love that has experienced abuse, false accusation, extreme loneliness, and immense pain. Good Friday shows us that God understands, and so, in our prayers, we can bring to him people and places where there is pain and suffering. God has experienced every kind of suffering we are likely to encounter. He knows and feels our pain, and one day he will remove it from the world. Meanwhile, he is with us in our suffering, he offers us his support, and he promises to bring good things from it.

Prayers

Ask the congregation to think of the people they know who need to know God's love. If appropriate, they could write their names on paper and put them at the foot of the cross:

Lord Jesus, on Good Friday you suffered so much.
We ask you to look with compassion on those we know who are in pain or suffering.
May they know your loving touch on their lives, and find in you the hope they need. Amen.

Song or music

Witnesses

Narrator: Finally we hear from the Roman officer on duty that day.

Centurion: I've overseen many executions. It's part of my job, but somehow this one was different. I actually heard this Jesus ask God to forgive us for what we were doing to him! It has changed the way I see things. I'm a Roman, but there was something about Jesus – something to do with God's love. I suddenly found myself understanding things in a new way, and I realised this really was God's son!

Song or music

Finish with a hymn and blessing.

Totally eclipsed

A service for Good Friday by Jonathan Mortimer

Songs

Opening hymn

'There is a green hill'; 'In Christ alone' (omit Easter verse)

During the service

'For God so loved the world'; 'I thank you for the cross'; 'Wonderful grace'; 'Who is there like you'; 'Here is love'; 'How deep the Father's love for us'; 'It's your blood that cleanses me'; 'You laid aside your majesty'

Closing hymn

'When I survey'; 'There is a redeemer'

Opening words

Jesus said 'I am the light for the world. Follow me, and you won't be walking in the dark. You will have the light that gives life.'
John 8:12

You could place a single candle, or other light, where it is visible to all.

Hymn/song

Introduction

Invite the congregation to look at a painting portraying Jesus – either copied onto OHT, PowerPoint or paper. It could be a Good Friday scene, but be sensitive, in your selection, to the range of ages which might be present. Alternatively have a simple cross at the front of church as the focus. After about 20 seconds make the point that, although everyone has looked at the same picture (or cross) what they actually 'saw' was different. Some may have found it boring, others fascinating; people may have found it sad, strangely attractive, awful or beautiful. Why is this? Because, although we all have the same light and we have the same picture/object in front of us, we see through different eyes. You could ask a few people for one-word reactions to the picture, or ask what they found most striking about it.

Explain that those present on Good Friday saw Jesus through different eyes. After you mention each of the following, someone in the congregation could read out the relevant verses:

- The chief priests saw him as an enemy (Mark 14:63,64).
- The crowd saw him as a suitable victim (15:12–14).
- Pilate saw him as a threat to his position (15:15).
- The soldiers saw him as a joke (15:19,20).

Prayer

Introduce this prayer by explaining the meaning of the word 'survey' in the first line of 'When I survey the wondrous cross'. Link it to the activity you have done, looking at the picture or cross. As you pray, the music of the hymn could be played.

Lord Jesus Christ, when we survey the wondrous cross, give us eyes to see who you truly are: the Prince of Glory, Lord and King, Ruler and Saviour. Where our picture of you is wrong, please change it by your Spirit working in us. Amen.

Bible reading

Mark 15:20b–32 with two people reading alternate paragraphs. They could stand at opposite sides of the church. At the end they should stay in position to do the second reading in the same way.

Hymn/song

Bible reading

Mark 15:33–41

Short talk (part I)

Have a line of actors wearing a variety of spectacles (these might be borrowed or bought from charity shops – but avoid anything that will appear comic). When the talk begins, their backs are to the congregation. Show again your picture or cross from the introduction. Ask how it might appear if we looked at it through different glasses, such as those here. *(The actors turn to face the congregation.)* Some would make the picture blurred (if you have an OHP, illustrate by adjusting the focus). Other lenses could make it appear smaller, or bring it closer. Sunglasses would make it darker. *(The actors turn round again and remain in place for the sketch on page 62.)*

Explain that on Good Friday, amongst the crowd who saw the crucifixion of Jesus, no one truly saw and understood what was happening. The darkness that covered the land (v 33) symbolised the evil that was blinding eyes and clouding vision. Even those there who loved Jesus, the women brave enough to stay at the cross, could not see. It was as though everyone was wearing the wrong glasses.

Hymn/song

Sketch

This drama is played in mime accompanied by appropriately harsh music.

As the music begins, the line of actors, still wearing glasses, turn round and mime that they are making fun of an imaginary victim.

An actor with no glasses enters. The music fades out. The newcomer is puzzled that the others are acting so cruelly. They try to persuade the newcomer to join in. Then one of them produces and hands over a spare pair of glasses. The newcomer tries them on and, as the music restarts, gradually joins in the mockery. The music stops suddenly and all freeze.

After a short pause, the music restarts. The actors now mime beating someone up. A second newcomer enters without glasses. Again the newcomer only joins in when they are handed glasses. The music stops again and all freeze.

When the music restarts a final time, the actors mime different reactions of hatred and mockery to the imaginary victim: mocking, punching, pointing, despising, spitting, whipping. When one actor (a Roman army officer) slowly removes their glasses, the music stops and everyone freezes. A narrator reads Mark 15:37,38, with the Roman army officer speaking the words: 'This man really was the Son of God!' He then sinks to his knees.

Short talk (part 2)

Describe how, as Jesus died on the cross, everything was surrounded by darkness. But in one person there was a tiny glimmer of light, which started to shine at that moment. Explain how this light wasn't physical light, but understanding. This one man, the unlikeliest imaginable, caught a glimmer of the truth about

Jesus. The Roman officer had seen many crucifixions, and was in charge of them today. But he had never seen anyone live their last moments and die like Jesus. He may have said more than he really understood in calling Jesus 'Son of God', but somehow, more than any of the others present, he had seen who this really was on the cross before them.

Like the crowd in the sketch, we can easily copy the ideas and actions of those around us. It's so easy to see only what others see; to believe what they believe; to act as they act. Jesus never said the words 'Follow me' to crowds. He said it to people one or two at a time. He said it to people who were ready to come out of the crowd and to get to know him as he really is; to look through new eyes at Jesus, at themselves and at others.

Explain that as we recognise who Jesus really is – God's beloved only Son – we see how costly his death for us was. Encourage the congregation with that amazing love – that God gave his only Son so we can be forgiven and put right with him.

Confession

It may be appropriate to play again the music of 'When I survey the wondrous cross' during this prayer of confession. Afterwards, you could have music playing or silence. Invite the congregation to stay and pray for as long as they wish before leaving quietly.

Lord God, we are sorry that we take on the attitudes of people around us without thinking. We need to know your truth. Because you love us... *forgive us and help us.*

Lord God, we are sorry that we do not value properly all that Jesus went through on the cross for us. We need you to change us. Because you love us... *forgive us and help us.*

Lord God, we are sorry that we do just what we want. We need your help so we can live for Jesus who died for us. Because you love us... *forgive us and help us.*

Lord God, give us eyes to see, ears to hear and hearts to understand your love poured out in our lives today. Amen.

Totally eclipsed

The greatest story ever told

An Easter Sunday service by Mary Hawes

Preparation

Before the service, darken your building as much as possible, covering or masking Easter flowers, banners and so on with easily removable covers. Play quiet, reflective music as people arrive, to create a sombre mood. (If your tradition is to process at the start of the service, delay it until the first hymn/song.)

Music

Opening hymns/songs

'Led like a lamb'; 'Jesus Christ is risen today'; 'Be still, for the presence of the Lord'; 'Wake up O sleeper'; 'Glory, glory in the highest'

During the service

'Lord let your glory fall'; 'Praise God from whom all blessings flow'; 'Lord you have my heart'; 'These are the days of Elijah'

Closing hymns/songs

'I believe in Jesus'; 'Lord, I lift your name on high'; 'My Jesus, my Saviour'; 'Jesus, God's righteousness revealed'

Introduction

Start the service (without any introductory welcome or notices) by reading Luke 23:50-56. To add atmosphere, add a slow drumbeat in the background. After a few minutes' silence, one (primed) person runs to the front and shouts, 'He's not dead! Jesus is risen!' This is the signal for some of the (primed) others to turn to their neighbours and say: 'Jesus is risen! Pass it on.' Two or three more people quickly remove the covers from the Easter decorations and musician(s) begin to play the opening song of praise, quietly at first, then gradually getting louder at which point the whole congregation is invited to join in. Turn the darkened atmosphere to light.

Praise

The leader says the lines questioningly; the congregation responds with 'Jesus is risen', getting louder and louder.

Leader: What's that you say?
People: Jesus is risen!
Leader: But he was dead!
People: Jesus is risen!
Leader: Nailed to a cross
People: Jesus is risen!
Leader: Laid in a grave
People: Jesus is risen!
Leader: Dead for three days
People: Jesus is risen!
Leader: Now he's alive?
People: Jesus is risen!
Leader: Death overcome?
People: Jesus is risen!
Leader: *(Triumphantly.)* Hope for us all!
People: Jesus is risen!
Leader: Shout with one voice:
People: Jesus is risen! Alleluia!

Bible reading

Luke 24:1-12. You could include the reading as part of the talk. If you require a second reading, one of the following may be helpful: Psalm 139:1-18; Revelation 21:1-5; 1 Corinthians 15:50-58.

All-age talk

You will need: five large 'stones' cut out of cardboard with a word on one side and a letter on the other: betrayed/R; arrested/I; crucified/S; buried/E; hopeless/N.

Narrator: It had been an amazing few days for Jesus' disciples. Just the week before, they had heard the crowds shouting Jesus' praise as he rode into Jerusalem. Now it seemed things had changed for ever. *(Ask for volunteers to hold up the 'stones' as you make the following points.)*

Betrayed. The religious leaders in Jerusalem wanted Jesus out of the way but they had been too scared of the crowds to do anything about it. And then Judas, one of Jesus' friends had betrayed him, telling the leaders where they could find him. Did the disciples feel that Jesus had betrayed them as well?

Arrested. Jesus had been arrested. The soldiers took him away from his friends. The disciples must have felt confused – what was happening to

The greatest story ever told

their friend, the man they believed to be God's promised Saviour? And if Jesus had been arrested, would they be next?

Crucified. Maybe it was all a mistake. Maybe the soldiers would let Jesus go – after all, he'd never done anything wrong. But no! The plot against Jesus continued. He was brought before the Roman Governor; people told lies about him – and Jesus was crucified alongside two thieves.

Buried. Surely Jesus couldn't be dead! Maybe he had survived the crucifixion, badly hurt but still alive. But no! When his friends took Jesus down from the cross, he was dead. They took his body and buried it in a rock tomb, and a large stone was placed across the entrance.

Hopeless. Two days later, as the women came to the tomb, everything must have seemed hopeless. Their Lord and Master, whom they had loved and followed, was dead and buried. All they could do now was bring spices to anoint him.

The first day of the week. Read Luke 24:1–12. *(If possible, have it read by someone out of sight.)* The women thought all hope of seeing Jesus again had gone. The last thing they expected to find was the stone rolled away and the tomb empty! But the angel told them that Jesus is *(Aask the volunteers to turn the 'stones' over.)* R-I-S-E-N, risen! The risen Jesus, through his Spirit, is with us. No matter how dark or hopeless things may seem, the message of Easter is that Jesus is always with us, giving us the hope of new beginnings.

Responding to God

Give each person a stone or pebble, or a stone shape cut out of paper. Ask people to look at their stone as they think of a situation which seems hopeless. Give one or two examples, such as a friendship which has gone wrong, a country where there is war or something that is affecting your particular gathering of Christians. As a resurrection hymn is played quietly, invite the congregation to bring their stones forward to lay at a focal point – an Easter garden, or the foot of a cross, maybe – as a sign of God's desire to roll away our stones of hopelessness and replace them with new beginnings.

Intercessions

Use these responses between prayers for the world, your locality and individual situations.

Where hope seems buried... *resurrected Lord, bring new life.*

Closing prayer

Almighty God, Father of the Lord Jesus Christ, we offer you our thanks and praise.
Because of your great mercy, you give us new life through the resurrection of your Son.
Fill us with your living hope, that in all times of joy and despair we may trust you, the one true God who makes all things new. Amen.
Based on 1 Peter 1:3-6.

A cracking time!

A service for Easter Sunday by Marjory Francis

Preparation

You will need: three large chocolate Easter eggs in their boxes, looking untouched. However, the contents of the eggs will have been removed beforehand and the following changes made: the first egg should contain contents different to and better than those the box says, the second a toy chick, and the third egg should be empty. You will also need a clean surface, a clean mallet or similar (the more flamboyant the better!), several paper plates and coloured pens (how many depends on the size of your congregation – see below)

Hymns/songs

'Jesus Christ is risen today'; 'Jesus Christ is alive today'; 'I believe in Jesus'; 'Sing a song, sing a joyful song'; 'Thine/Yours be the glory.'

Songs could also be sung between the sections of the talk.

Easter shout

Welcome everyone to your Easter service. Ask them to think of a short word or phrase that expresses our joy on this day, eg 'Alleluia!' or 'Jesus is alive!' (Suggestions could be displayed on a screen.) Ask everyone to say their chosen phrase to the person next to them. Then ask them to call it out to someone nearby or along the row. Then ask them to shout it out to someone across the room.

Song

Tell everyone that during your first song, paper plates and pens will be passed round. Adults and older children can write their phrase and smaller children can make a representative mark on the plate. Collect the plates.

Confession

Remind everyone that when Jesus came back to life on the first Easter day, he showed that, through his death on the cross, our sins could be forgiven. We can confidently come to him for forgiveness. Ask everyone to think quietly for a few moments about the things they need forgiveness for. Then ask them to join in the response:

Lord Jesus, we are sorry for the wrong things we have done.

Thank you that you died on the cross...
So that I can be forgiven.

Lord Jesus, we are sorry for the wrong things we have looked at...
So that I can be forgiven.

Lord Jesus, we are sorry for the wrong things we have listened to...
So that I can be forgiven.

Lord Jesus, we are sorry for the wrong things we have thought...
So that I can be forgiven.

Lord Jesus, we are sorry for not loving and serving you as we should...
So that I can be forgiven.

Song

Reading

Ask 'What's Easter all about?', inviting responses particularly from the children in the congregation. Say 'Let's see what the Bible says about this day 2,000 years ago.' Have Luke 24:1–12 read by two voices, one saying the words of the men in white.

Talk

Introduction

The reading is a bit of a puzzle, isn't it? What was happening? Lots of bewildered people expecting one thing and finding another – and what did they find? Well, we have some puzzles today too. Make a show of putting your three eggs on display. What are we going to find?

Tell everyone that you are going to have a cracking time, then get out your mallet, waving it around flamboyantly.

A cracking time!

Empty!

Unwrap the first and fanciest egg, making a big show of reading out what should be in the egg. Invite a child to crack this one open. What's inside? Nothing. Precisely: it is completely empty, just as the cave on that Sunday morning long ago was empty – the proof that Jesus was indeed alive again. Later of course, Jesus' friends met him – in the garden, along the road, on the beach. But for now, their proof was the empty tomb. Many people over the years have found that the empty tomb was for them the first evidence that Jesus rose from the dead. Then they have gone on to meet him too, in the garden, along the road, on the beach and in many other places. (After each section allow the child to eat one piece of chocolate and share the rest out onto the paper plates decorated earlier.)

New life

Unwrap the second egg, again reading what should be inside. Invite a child to come and crack it open. Discover the chick inside. Say: 'Well, what else would you expect in an egg?' This is a time of new life. In our spring gardens we find new life everywhere, but the new life of Easter is even more exciting. When Jesus' women friends went to the tomb with their spices, they were not expecting to find life at all. But as the angels said: 'Why are you looking in the place of the dead for someone who is alive?' We're thinking about the new life Jesus had, which means we can have new life too.

A surprise

Unwrap the third, most unpromising egg, reading the box aloud and remarking specifically about the [supposed] contents. Invite a child to crack the egg open with the mallet. Express deep surprise that what it said on the box is not what you have found inside; it is something better. Say that God loves to surprise us, and he gives us so much more than we could ever imagine. On the Sunday morning we are reading about, Jesus' friends were expecting to find a dead body. What God gave them was the most wonderful surprise ever. This is what God gives us too, something far better than we could ever imagine – a new life because Jesus died and is alive again! Encourage the congregation to shout their praise shouts again.

Prayer

Suggest that you thank Jesus together for his new life and what it means, and pray for those who have not met him yet.

We thank you, Father God, that you raised your Son Jesus from death, and that his life means that we too can live with him for evermore. We pray for those who haven't yet discovered that he is alive today, and we pray that they will know the evidence of the empty tomb and meet with him.

Song

During this song, ask some of the older children to pass the plates of chocolate pieces around the congregation.

Blessing

May the God of everlasting life, Father, Son and Holy Spirit, bless us today and always.

Jesus comes back to life

A Key Stage 1 assembly for Easter by Heather Butler

Bible base: Luke 23:26–56; John 20:1–18

Aim: to think about Easter eggs and Easter celebrations; to hear what Christians believe happened on the first Easter; and to reflect on what happened.

Introduction

Talk about Easter eggs, what's inside them and why we have them.

Easter eggs are a sign of new life, just like when a chick hatches out of an egg. Christians believe that Jesus came back to life after he was killed.

Story

Jesus had been in Jerusalem for several days and was with his special friends, his disciples. The soldiers came for him very late at night when not many people were around. All Jesus' friends ran away and left him on his own. He was taken to see a very important person called Pilate. Pilate blamed Jesus for causing a lot of trouble even though he hadn't done anything wrong. He then said Jesus should die.

The soldiers led Jesus away. They made him carry a huge cross made out of wood over his shoulders. Jesus kept falling over because the cross was so heavy and he was so tired.

The soldiers saw a man called Simon. They grabbed hold of him and made him carry Jesus' cross. Two other men, who were robbers, were there as well, carrying their wooden crosses. Finally, they reached a hill outside the city. They had to lie down on the wood, and nails were hammered through their hands and feet so they could be hung up on the crosses. The soldiers laughed at Jesus. He could have come down off the cross if he had wanted to, but he chose not to.

At about twelve o'clock, in the middle of the day, darkness spread right over the land. It went completely black, as if it was night-time, and stayed like that for three hours.

Then Jesus cried out in a loud voice. 'Father,' he said, 'I put myself in your hands!' And then he died.

Later on, a man called Joseph went to Pilate and asked him if he could have Jesus' body. Joseph took the body down, wrapped it in a linen sheet and placed it in a tomb. (A tomb is a hole dug out of a rock where bodies are put.) Then a large stone was rolled across the entrance to the tomb so that no one could get in or out.

All that happened on a Friday. It's now known as Good Friday. Very early on Sunday morning, Jesus' friend, Mary, went to the tomb. She had the biggest shock of her life because the stone that had covered the entrance to the tomb had gone!

Mary thought someone had stolen Jesus' body and began to cry. After a while she saw someone else in the garden with her. 'If you took him away,' she said, 'tell me where you have put him.'

'Mary!' the man said.

Mary gasped. She knew that voice. It was Jesus. He had died, but he had come back to life again.

Thinking time...

Christians believe that Jesus died. They also believe that he came back to life again. Only someone who was God could do that. Think of one word that will remind you of what Christians believe happened at Easter. See if you can remember that as you eat any Easter eggs this year.

Prayer

Dear God, thank you for Easter eggs, but thank you even more that you love us enough to let your son, Jesus, be born as a baby and live on this earth. Thank you that he died and then came back to life again.
Amen.

(First published in Creative Assemblies, *SU)*

What are you like?

A Key Stage 2 assembly for Easter by Andrew Smith

Bible base: Luke 18:9–14

Aim: To teach children that Easter is a time when Christians think about the wrong things they've done and remember that God forgives sin.

You will need: paper and pencils, The body quiz, two large body outlines drawn on paper and cut up, Blu-Tack, music and CD player (optional).

Introduction

Ask for a couple of volunteers who like to draw. Give them pencils and paper, and tell them they have about three minutes to draw a self-portrait. Whilst they are doing that, divide the rest of the children into two teams and do the 'Body quiz'. When a team gets a question right, they can stick a body part to the wall. The first team to make a body wins. Select questions appropriate for the school and the age level of the children.

Self portraits

After the quiz, look at the self-portraits and see how accurate they are. Congratulate the artists on their efforts. Point out how hard it is to draw a self-portrait, especially without a mirror, as we often forget what we look like. In fact there are lots of things we don't know about ourselves.

The Pharisee and the tax collector

Tell the children that in the Bible there is a story Jesus told about two people. One thought he knew everything about himself. Ask the pupils to listen carefully as you tell the story and see if they can spot which man knew most about himself. Tell the parable of the Pharisee and Tax Collector (Luke 18:9–14). Ask a couple of students to act out the story as you tell it.

When you have finished, ask the pupils which of the men knew most about himself. Why? Explain that it was the tax collector, because he knew he was sinful (briefly explain 'sinful' if necessary). But the Pharisee couldn't see his own faults. Jesus went on to say that it was the tax collector who would be forgiven because he wasn't proud, but was honest about what he was like.

Application

A Christian viewpoint

The Easter festival is a special time for Christians to think about the wrong things they've done and to ask God to forgive them. Easter is when Christians remember that Jesus died for the wrong things people have done. It's a time to be honest about what we're really like and to ask God to forgive us. The Bible says it's important for Christians to be honest and admit to God the wrong things they've done, and not pretend that they're perfect.

For everyone

Everyone does things wrong, but often we don't want to admit it. We know other people do things wrong, but don't want to see faults in ourselves. Sometimes we don't seem to know ourselves very well.

Response

In a short time of quiet, ask the children to think about things they've done which they know are wrong. You could play some quiet music at this point. Encourage the students to think if there's anyone they need to be honest with or say sorry to: themselves, other people, or perhaps God. Finish with this prayer, offering them the chance to opt out by not saying 'Amen', but sitting quietly and thinking about the issue.

Dear Lord, we know that often we do things wrong. Please help us to know when we've done wrong, and to be brave enough to say sorry. We want to say sorry now for times when we've done things which have upset other people and you. Please forgive us and help us not to do those things again. Amen.

The body quiz

1 How many hearts have you got? (*One.*)
2 Name the five senses. (*Hearing, sight, smell, taste, touch.*)
3 Which teeth are used to grind up food? (*Molars.*)
4 What does the heart do? (*Pumps blood around the body.*)
5 Why do we need bones? (*To provide a rigid structure for our bodies; to enable us to move.*)
6 Which is the longest bone in the human body? (*The thigh bone.*)
7 In what does the blood travel round the body? (*Blood vessels – arteries, capillaries and veins.*)
8 What are the lungs used for? (*To supply the body with oxygen and to expel carbon dioxide from the body.*)
9 Where would you find the cochlea? (*The ear.*)
10 What makes someone short-sighted? (*The eye is too long from front to back, so that it doesn't focus properly.*)

(First published in Everyone Can Know, SU)

Egg race

A Key Stage 3 assembly for Easter by Andy Banks

Bible base: John 11:25,26

Aim: To help students learn more about the meaning of Easter.

You will need: three Cadbury's Crème Eggs (or similar), an advert for Cadbury's Crème Eggs (or similar), a stopwatch, mini-chocolate eggs – enough for one for everyone in the assembly (optional, depending on the school and your finances!).

Preparation

Find out, if possible, the current 'world record' for time taken to eat a Cadbury's Crème Egg, or have a suitable other 'record' ready (eg from other schools, youth groups etc visited).

Introduction

Ask the students some questions about Easter eggs, eg 'Who likes chocolate?'; 'How many Easter eggs did you get last year?' Show an advert for Crème Eggs. Show them a Cadbury's Crème Egg – hinting that someone in this assembly might get the egg!

Going for the record

Say that the 'record' time taken to eat a Crème Egg is... Ask if anyone thinks they could beat that. Ask for two volunteers (who like Crème Eggs!). Give them both a Crème Egg and challenge them to see who can eat their egg in the shorter time. Will either of them beat the record? Tell them they are not allowed to swallow the egg whole.

Use a stop-watch for timing. Make sure that both competitors start at the same time, on your 'Go!' Encourage support for both, making sure that both volunteers have support! You could ask half the audience to support one competitor, and the other half the other one. Build up the atmosphere by commentating as the contest develops. Cheer the winner. Announce the times. Is there a new record? Award the winner another egg as their prize.

Reflection

Comment that it's great getting, and eating, Easter eggs, but what's the point of them? Ask the students to suggest some answers. Then respond to answers given. These might include:

- New life
- Baby chicks being born
- Spring/new life beginning
- Jesus coming back to life

Talk briefly about the answers you receive, making sure that the above are included. Then go on to explain that Christians believe Jesus' death and resurrection – his coming back to life – mean that forgiveness, new life and the chance to start again are possible for everyone.

Response

In a time of quiet, ask students to think about:

- What does Easter mean to me?
- Are there any ways in which I need to make a new start?

Pray, if appropriate, and then wish everyone 'Happy Easter'!

Optional extra: Tell the students that you're going to give them each a mini-Easter egg as they leave. As they eat it, ask them to think about anything they need forgiveness for, or ways in which they need to make a fresh start. Say that they could even ask God to help them with that. (Make sure you encourage them to put the wrapping in a rubbish bin!)

(First published in Flatpack, *SU)*

Creative prayer for Easter

Welcoming Jesus

A prayer of welcome for Palm Sunday

Explain that when Jesus entered Jerusalem the people shouted praises to welcome him. As the people greeted Jesus, we can also respond to him and give him praise. Use the responsive prayer below, encouraging everyone to respond loudly with the words in italics.

In our town and in our homes,
We welcome you, Jesus!
With our friends and families,
We welcome you, Jesus!

In our work and play,
We welcome you, Jesus!
In all that we hope for,
We welcome you, Jesus!

In the times when we are upset or worried,
We welcome you, Jesus!
In every part of our lives,
We welcome you, Jesus!

Palm-leaf prayers

A creative prayer for Palm Sunday

You will need: green paper palm-leaf shapes, pens, brown-paper tree trunk, backing paper, glue

Read the words of praise that the crowd shouted as Jesus rode into town (John 12:12,13). Encourage everyone to write their own one-line praise prayers on the palm leaves, eg 'Jesus, you're amazing!', 'Jesus, you're the best friend ever!'

Mount the brown palm-tree trunk onto backing paper. Paste all the palm-leaf prayers around the top to make a prayer collage.

Palm Sunday praise

An action prayer for Palm Sunday

Divide the congregation into four groups, giving each group a phrase from Luke 19:38: 'Blessed is the king'; 'who comes in the name of the Lord'; 'Peace in heaven'; 'and glory to God'.

As each group calls out their phrase, they stand up and then sit down again as the next group stands and calls out their phrase, creating a 'Mexican wave' effect. After a practise, run through the shout of praise three times and then lead straight into a song of praise.

King Jesus

A prayer of confession suitable for Palm Sunday

Encourage the congregation to join in with the response line in italics.

Lord, we confess that sometimes we have not welcomed you as our king,
King Jesus, forgive us, and rule in our hearts.

Lord, we confess that sometimes we have disowned you.
King Jesus, forgive us, and rule in our hearts.

Lord, we confess that sometimes we have not loved people as you commanded us to do.
King Jesus, forgive us, and rule in our hearts.

Lord, we confess that sometimes we have not followed your example and served others.
*King Jesus, forgive us, and rule in our hearts.
Amen.*

Receive our welcome

A responsive prayer for Palm Sunday

Encourage the congregation to join in with the response line in italics.

Lord Jesus, you rode into Jerusalem in triumph, receiving the shouts and welcome of many.
Come into this church today.
Receive our welcome and our acclaim.

Lord Jesus, you rode into Jerusalem in triumph, and you irritated the proud and self-important.
Come into this church today.
Soften our hearts and our attitudes.

Lord Jesus, you rode into Jerusalem in triumph, and you began the events of a week that changed the world.
Come into this church today.
Change our world. You are the king.

Gift of praise

A prayer of praise for Palm Sunday

Make a gift of praise for Jesus the king. Gift wrap a large box and tie a bright ribbon around it. Then give out sticky labels and ask the congregation to write or draw something they want to praise God for. Play some music while people come up to fix their praises on to the box.

In the crowd

A meditation for Palm Sunday

As the song 'From heaven you came' (The Servant King) is played softly, ask the congregation to imagine themselves in the crowd in Jerusalem that day. Picture the scene; imagine the sounds and smells. Now, as Jesus rides past you, are you one of those laying your cloak or a palm branch in front of him? Is your voice joining the shouts of the others? Are you simply excited about following the crowd? Or do you know that this is the Servant King riding for your sake to die on a cross? If we recognise who Jesus is, we have to be willing for him to change us by his gentle presence in our lives.

Sing 'Spirit of the living God, fall afresh on me', and invite people to come forward to receive a palm cross as a sign of accepting Jesus as their King.

Torn in two

An active prayer of response suitable for Good Friday.

You will need: a short length of ribbon for each person, a curtain torn in two

Invite everyone to pin their piece of ribbon to the 'torn' curtain to represent the sin that gets between them and God. In a large church, have a few people doing this on behalf of everyone. Lead a prayer of confession, then thank God for destroying all those barriers through Jesus' death.

Pray, together if possible:

Be with us, Lord, in the seeking and the finding. Draw near us, Lord, in the stumbling and the falling. Reveal yourself to us, in the gazing and the loving. Amen.

At the close of the service, invite people to walk through the gap in the curtain as a sign of coming freely to God.

Five senses

A prayer for Easter Sunday

Depending on the make up of the congregation, you could do actions while saying this prayer together.

Thank you God for the taste of the tears, Tears that changed to smiles, because Jesus is alive.

Thank you God for the smell of the perfumes, Perfumes that were not needed, because Jesus is alive.

Thank you God for when they saw, That the cave was empty, because Jesus is alive.

Thank you God for when they touched, Their faces to the ground, because Jesus is alive.

Thank you God that they heard, The best news of their lives, because Jesus is alive.

Thank you God that we can sing and dance and shout and laugh, because Jesus is alive.

Colour coded

An Easter prayer incorporating a simple craft activity

You will need: A4 papers in different colours (see below), drawing materials, stapler

Remind everyone that, for those who loved Jesus, Good Friday was a dreadful day when very bad things happened, Saturday was a quiet, sad day and Sunday, a wonderful day of rejoicing.

Give each person a dark paper for Friday, a neutral coloured paper for Saturday and a bright paper for Sunday. Let them write the days at the top, then draw or write about events of each day on the appropriate sheet. Use white, silver or yellow crayon on the dark paper. Staple the sheets together in order.

Say that the three different days were all part of God's plan. With the Friday pages showing, pray thanking God that Jesus died on the cross so that we could be forgiven. Turn to Saturday and allow a time of quiet to think about how much God loves us, then turn to Sunday and invite everyone to shout their own praises to Jesus for being alive today.

Light triumphs

A prayer experience for the Easter period

You will need: a relighting candle (test it at home first), box of matches

Light the candle and talk about Jesus' death as the darkness trying to put out the light (Jesus). Blow the candle out. As it relights, say that Jesus' power was greater than the darkness and he came back to life.

Say the following prayer, with everyone joining in with the response:

Thank you, Jesus, for your love for us.
Hallelujah! Jesus is the King!

Thank you for suffering so that we can have new life.
Hallelujah! Jesus is the King!

We praise you because you defeated death.
Hallelujah! Jesus is the King!

Help us to know you are close to us always.
Hallelujah! Jesus is the King! Amen.

Roll away the stone

A closing prayer for Easter Sunday

Risen Lord Jesus,
Roll away the stone of our doubts;
Let us trust you.
Roll away the stone of our reserve;
Let us proclaim you.
Roll away the stone of our heaviness of heart;
Let us rejoice in you.
Roll away the stone of our fear;
Let us find hope in you,
Now and through all eternity. Amen.

Living in the light

A responsive prayer for the Easter period

Ask two readers to read the following sentences, with the congregation responding with the words in italics.

A: The stone is rolled away; Jesus is no longer dead.
Jesus of Nazareth who was crucified has risen!
B: Lord, help us to live in the light of your truth.

A: God has made this Jesus both Lord and Christ.
Jesus of Nazareth who was crucified has risen!
B: Lord, help us to live in the light of your truth.

A: Jesus Christ is the same yesterday, and today and for ever.
Jesus of Nazareth who was crucified has risen!
B: Lord, help us to live in the light of your truth.

All stand up

A game which challenges children to think about the Easter story

Ask the children to think of a word associated with the Easter season (eg Jesus, Peter, Mary, cross, alive, resurrection). They keep their word a secret, but make sure they remember it. If you think younger children will have difficulty thinking of or remembering their word, put them in pairs with older children.

When everyone has thought of a word, they should stand up. Wait for all the children to stand.

Now the leaders have to guess the words. As you make a guess, whichever children chose that word have to sit down. They should be able to explain what their word has to do with the Easter story.

The last child or pair standing wins when they reveal their relevant word.

Go for it!

A game which celebrates the good news of Easter.

You will need: a set of the letters of 'Jesus is risen' for each team (each team's in a different colour), Easter eggs to share

Spread the letters, all mixed-up, on a table or floor at one end of the room. Divide the children into teams, line them up and tell them which colour they are. The children go in turn to collect a letter of their colour. The next child cannot go until the previous child is back and has put the letter down in a designated place, eg on a chair.

When all their letters have been collected, the team must put them in order for a very important message. The first team to have all their letters in order wins.

Let the winning team read out the words, then read them all together. Share the Easter eggs with all the teams as a prize for taking part.

Today's news

A non-competitive game to introduce the Easter story

You will need: lots of egg shapes cut from newspaper, thick coloured pens, the words 'Jesus is alive!' written up to copy, recorded music

Spread the egg shapes over the floor. Say that they are covered with the news – but we have some better news today! Give each child a coloured pen. Play the music as the children move and dance between the egg shapes. When the music stops they can write on one of the shapes 'Jesus is alive!' Keep moving to the music and writing until all the shapes have the new news on them. Finish by saying that we are going to hear the story of that great news today.

Sort the fish

An active game based on the resurrection appearance in John 21

You will need: 153 fish shapes in four different colours or four different shapes (see page 75), four buckets, a watch with a second hand

Before the game, cut out 153 fish in four different colours/shapes. Put the four buckets (these are 'nets') around the room.

Explain to the children that you have four different types of fish, which need sorting into the right nets. Explain which 'net' is for which colour/shape. Spread the fish out in the middle of the room and challenge the children to sort the fish in a limited amount of time. The time needed will depend on the size of your group. The children are allowed to carry only one fish at a time.

Play the game more than once, challenging the children to improve on the time they take. Afterwards, ask the children to put the fish into piles of ten and to count them. Together, look up John 21:11 to see if they have counted correctly. Tell the story of how Jesus appeared to his disciples from John 21.

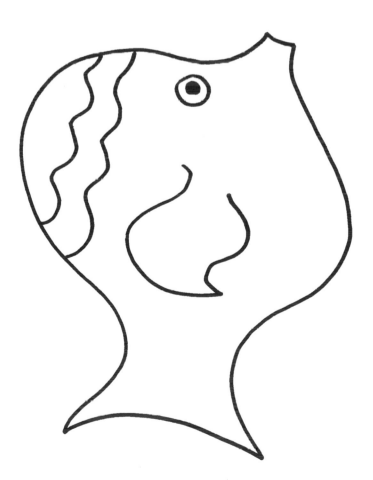

Charoseth

A traditional part of the Passover meal

You will need: (This amount makes four small balls, so multiply the ingredients as necessary.) An eating apple; a dessertspoonful of sultanas; some chopped almonds; pinch of cinnamon; sugar

Peel and finely grate the apple. Mix all the other ingredients and add to the grated apple. Roll the mixture into balls and sprinkle with sugar.

Unleavened bread

Bread made without yeast for a Passover meal.

You will need: 1 cup flour; 1/3 cup water; salt; olive oil

Preheat the oven to Gas mark 7, 220ºC and place two baking sheets in the oven to heat through. Dust the work surface and a rolling pin with a little flour. Measure the flour into a mixing bowl. Gradually add the water to the flour, stirring rapidly with a fork. Form the dough into a ball, and knead for about 30 seconds until the dough is smooth. Divide the dough into four pieces. Form each piece into a ball. Flatten the ball between your hands, then place on the lightly floured surface.

First roll each piece into a 5 inch pancake shape. Then roll them out further in turn to 8 inches in diameter. (It's important to allow the dough to rest between rollings.) Prick the dough several times all over. Remove the preheated baking sheets.

Place the flattened rounds of dough on the preheated baking sheet, and place on rack near the top of the oven. Bake for 2 minutes on each side until the bread is lightly brown and crisp. Transfer to a wire rack to cool. Sprinkle with olive oil and salt to taste.

Simnel cake

A traditional Easter cake from the United Kingdom

You will need: 150 g margarine or butter; 150 g sugar; finely grated rind of 1 lemon; 2 eggs beaten; 200 g self-raising flour; 1/2 teaspoon mixed spice; 500 g dried fruit (sultanas, currants, raisins); 2 tablespoons milk; 750 g marzipan (warning: contains nuts); egg white to glaze; cornflour to dust

Cream the butter and sugar until the mixture is pale and fluffy. Add the lemon rind and beat in the eggs. Sift in the flour and mixed spice. Stir in the dried fruit and milk. Put half the mixture into an 18 cm (7 inch) deep baking tin which has been greased and lined with a double layer of greaseproof paper. Roll out a third of the marzipan to make a 15 cm (6 inch) circle (using the cornflour to dust the work surface). Place this in the baking tin and cover with the remaining mixture. Make a shallow hollow at the centre. Bake for 1 hour at gas mark 3, 170ºC, then lower the oven temperature to Gas mark 2, 150ºC and bake for another 1 1/4 hours. Turn out onto a wire rack, remove the paper and leave to cool. The cake is decorated with half the remaining marzipan, rolled out to fit the top of the cake. Brush the cake with egg white before laying the marzipan on top of it. Brush the top with egg white. The remaining marzipan is rolled into 11 balls (to represent the apostles who saw Jesus alive) and placed in a circle on top of the cake. Brush the balls with egg white and place the cake under a hot grill until the balls turn golden. Leave to cool completely.

Easter nests

An easy recipe to make with children

You will need: 50 g chocolate; 2 tablespoons golden syrup; 75 g puffed rice cereal; paper cases; miniature chocolate eggs

Put the chocolate and golden syrup into a bowl over a pan of simmering water and stir until melted. (Alternatively, microwave for a few seconds.) Cool a little before allowing children to touch the bowl. Mix in the puffed rice cereal. Spoon the mixture into the paper cases, shaping each cake into a nest. Put miniature eggs into the nests and allow to cool.

Recipes for Easter

Hot cross buns

This easy recipe produces 12 square buns marked with a pastry cross

You will need: 400 g strong plain flour; 1 teaspoon salt; 1 packet of dried yeast; 1/2 pint warm water; 1/2 teaspoon mixed spice; 50 g sugar; 50 g margarine; 1 egg; 50 g currants; 50 g sultanas; 100 g shortcrust pastry

Mix all the ingredients together thoroughly and knead for about 10 minutes. Put the dough into a greased tin measuring 30x24 cms (12x9 inches). Mark the dough into 12 equal buns and leave to rise for about an hour. Roll the pastry into strips and place across the dough so that each bun has a cross. Bake for 20 minutes at Gas mark 5 190°C. When the buns are still hot, glaze them with a tablespoon of sugar mixed with 4 tablespoons of water.

Easter biscuits

These delicious biscuits require a little skill, but are suitable for older children to make

You will need: 125 g butter; 75 g caster sugar; 1 egg, beaten; 225 g plain flour; 1/2 teaspoon mixed spice; 1/2 teaspoon ground cinnamon; 50g currants; 50 g cut mixed peel; caster sugar to dredge

Beat the butter and sugar in a bowl until light and creamy. Gradually beat in the egg. Carefully mix in the sifted flour and spices, and then the currants and peel to make a firm dough. Dust hands with flour and knead lightly. Roll out the dough on a lightly floured surface to about 6 mm thick and cut into 10 cm rounds with a cutter. Place the biscuits on lightly greased baking sheets (you will need several). Knead and roll out the trimmings and cut out more rounds until the dough is used up. Bake the biscuits in a preheated oven (Gas Mark 5, 190°C) for 15 minutes until lightly browned. Dredge with caster sugar and transfer to a wire rack to cool.

Koulibiac

A Russian fish dish eaten at Easter time. It could form the centrepiece of a shared meal in the Easter period

You will need: 800 g flaky pastry; tin of salmon or tuna (drained); 100 g long grain rice (cooked); 100 g chopped onion (fried); 50 g sliced mushrooms (fried); chopped parsley; rind and juice of half a lemon; salt and pepper; 2 hard-boiled eggs (chopped); 1 beaten egg

Roll out the pastry in two halves, both the same size and shape. Mix together the cooked rice, onion, mushrooms, parsley and lemon. Put half this mixture onto the pastry, leaving a margin all around the edge. Add a layer of half the fish; sprinkle over half the chopped egg, the rest of the fish and finally the rest of the rice mixture. Cover with the other half of pastry and seal the edges together. Score a few small cuts in the pastry for steam to be released. Glaze with beaten egg. Bake for 20 minutes in a moderately hot oven (Gas mark 6, 200°C). When cooled, dust with icing sugar.

Palm Sunday quiz

Twelve quiz questions based on Mark 11:1-11

1. What were the names of the two villages which Jesus arrived at? (Bethany and Bethphage.)

2. What was the nearest hill? (Mount of Olives.)

3. Getting closer to Jerusalem, how many disciples did Jesus send on ahead? (Two.)

4. Jesus told them to go into Jerusalem. True or false? (False - into the village.)

5. What would they find there? (A young donkey.)

6. This was the donkey which had previously been a winner in the Jerusalem donkey derby. Yes or no? (No - never been ridden.)

7. If they were questioned about the donkey, what were they to say? (The Lord needs it.)

8. Where was the donkey tied? (Near a door facing the street.)

9. How did the disciples dress the donkey? (Put clothes on its back.)

10. How and who littered the streets in an environmentally friendly way? (The crowd of people spread branches.)

11. What did the crowd shout about Jesus? (That he was coming in the name of the Lord.)

12. Which ancestor of Jesus did they shout about? (King David.)

True or false?

An Easter quiz which reviews the Easter story up to the burial of Jesus' body. It could be used as an active game in a room with one wall labelled 'True' and another 'False'. Participants run to the wall which they think has the correct answer.

1. Jesus rode into Jerusalem on a horse. (False - A donkey.)

2. The people cheered, waving palm branches. (True.)

3. Jesus spent the next ten days teaching the people. (False - He died five days later.)

4. Jesus celebrated the Passover meal with his 12 disciples. (True.)

5. Jesus washed his disciples' feet. (True.)

6. Jesus didn't know which of the disciples would betray him. (False - Jesus predicted Judas' betrayal during the Passover meal.)

7. Jesus was sentenced to death by the High Priest. (False - He could not pass the death sentence without the Roman governor.)

8. The Jews wanted Jesus to be set free. (False - They wanted Barabbas set free.)

9. One of Jesus' disciples, Judas Iscariot, committed suicide. (True.)

10. Jesus was too weak to carry his cross to the place of crucifixion. (True.)

11 Jesus was buried in his family tomb. (False - Joseph of Arimathea's tomb.)

12. The tomb was guarded by Roman soldiers. (True.)

Quizzes for Easter

We have seen the Lord!

Twelve questions about the resurrection stories

1. Why were the women going to the place where Jesus had been buried? (To anoint his body.)

2. Name one of the women. (Mary, Mary Magdalene, Salome or Joanna.)

3. Why didn't the women have to roll away the stone at the entrance of the tomb? (It was already rolled away.)

4. Which two disciples were the first to go to the tomb? (Peter and John.)

5. What did these two disciples find rolled up inside the tomb on Easter day? (The cloth that had been used to cover Jesus' face.)

6. Whom did Mary Magdalene mistake for a gardener outside the tomb? (Jesus.)

7. Two of Jesus' friends were walking home when Jesus appeared to them. Where did they live? (Emmaus.)

8. When Jesus appeared to his disciples when they were gathered together, what did they give him to eat? (A piece of cooked fish.)

9. Which disciple would not believe that Jesus was alive until he himself had touched the wounds in his hands and side? (Thomas.)

10. While waiting for Jesus in Galilee, which of Jesus' friends suggested they should go fishing? (Peter.)

11. With the help of Jesus, how many fish did they catch? (153.)

12. What did Jesus give them to eat for breakfast? (Bread and fish.)

Order time

Give teams the ten following statements (based on John 20:19-29) already cut into strips. The first team to place them in the right order wins!

A Jesus showed Thomas his scars and told him to stop doubting.

B The disciples told Thomas that they had seen Jesus alive.

C Jesus showed his disciples the scars on his hands and side.

D A week later, Jesus appeared to his disciples again. Thomas was there.

E The disciples were gathered behind locked doors.

F One of the twelve disciples, Thomas, was not present when Jesus came.

G Thomas answered, 'My Lord and my God.'

H The disciples became very happy.

I Thomas doubted them and said he needed to see the scars for himself before he could believe.

J Jesus breathed on the disciples and they received the Holy Spirit.

The correct sequence is: E, C, H, J, F, B, I, D, A, G

Spot the difference answers (page 82)

Easter wordsearch

G	A	R	D	S	C	O	E	E	A	S	T	E	R	L	M
H	U	A	V	E	U	V	L	K	L	B	A	N	D	L	A
E	E	A	Y	N	R	I	G	I	I	C	E	K	S	B	B
R	U	P	R	R	T	C	M	S	V	I	C	T	O	R	Y
O	I	H	P	H	A	R	I	S	E	E	J	F	R	W	R
D	I	R	E	U	I	H	G	B	O	W	S	S	P	A	U
K	I	E	F	L	N	R	O	B	B	N	T	O	B	D	Y
I	E	S	R	G	Y	I	C	N	Z	N	N	E	S	I	R
S	N	U	C	E	Z	A	S	T	L	E	P	P	E	P	A
P	A	R	J	I	T	L	U	H	X	V	V	L	H	U	M
B	M	R	E	B	P	E	P	O	M	A	Z	A	D	N	C
A	E	E	R	J	T	L	P	M	B	E	I	I	R	I	U
R	S	C	U	E	E	D	E	A	T	H	N	R	A	G	R
A	H	T	S	S	B	L	R	S	L	A	N	T	U	A	H
B	T	I	T	U	A	A	N	G	B	M	O	T	G	R	T
B	E	O	M	S	B	E	L	O	L	I	C	S	I	D	A
V	G	N	U	B	E	E	S	T	O	N	E	R	V	E	B
L	P	R	A	D	G	I	C	R	O	S	N	L	O	N	B
S	E	S	L	N	W	O	R	C	E	M	T	M	A	S	A
J	U	D	A	S	R	Y	D	P	I	L	A	T	E	S	S

EASTER	PRIEST	INNOCENT	THOMAS
CROSS	PHARISEE	PUNISHMENT	CROWN
PALM	PILATE	OLIVES	GRAVE
JESUS	RESURRECTION	DISCIPLES	RISEN
SUPPER	JERUSALEM	KISS	GETHSEMANE
JUDAS	BARABBAS	BETRAY	GARDEN
MARY	HEAVEN	DEATH	GUARD
TOMB	ANGEL	SON	TRIAL
PETER	STONE	ALIVE	SABBATH
HEROD	VICTORY	CURTAIN	GOD

Garden anguish

A puzzle suitable for adults and older children with good reading ability

You will need: Bibles, and copy of puzzle below for each person or pair

Give out Bibles and read Matthew 26:36–56 together. Invite everyone to answer the questions on the photocopied sheet, filling in the grids with their answers. Get them to complete the puzzle by transferring letters as numbered, so that they can answer the question about Jesus' prayer.

Get back together and ask what the answer to the puzzle means. Ask what the 'cup' represents. Explain that Jesus knew he was about to die, but he did not run away. He wished to avoid suffering, but more than anything else, he wanted to do God's will.

1 What was the name of the garden?

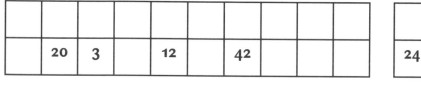

	20	3		12		42			

2 What did Jesus ask the disciples to do?

24	7	

3 What did Jesus do?

27	40	18	

4 When Jesus returned, what were the disciples doing?

		15	34		9		

5 Jesus said the disciples were…

	44		19	

6 How many times did Jesus return?

21	4	35	16	

7 Who did Jesus say he was being handed over to?

11	36		37	5		

8 Who betrayed Jesus?

	26		2	30

9 Whose servant had his ear cut off?

22	13	38				6	23			17

Slot the letters with numbers below them into the correct places to find out what Jesus prayed. What does this mean?

1	2	3	4	5	6
F					

7	8
	F

9	10	11	12	13	14	15	16
O					B		

17	18	19	20

21	22	23	24

25	26	27
C		

28	29
O	F

30	31	32	33	34	35	36	37	38
	U	F	F					

39	40	41	42
F		O	

43	44
M	

Puzzles

There are ten differences to find!

Easter 'Who's who?'

A matching activity

Join the names to the part they played in the Easter story.

Pilate

Peter

Joanna

Joseph from Arimathea

Herod

Judas

Simon from Cyrene

The high priest

A friend who betrayed Jesus.
Luke 22:47-48

Jesus was taken to his house after being arrested.
Luke 22:54

Denied he knew Jesus.
Luke 22:57

Asked Jesus, 'Arc you the King of the Jews?'
Luke:23:3

Asked Jesus many questions and mocked him.
Luke 23:9-11

Was made to carry Jesus' cross.
Luke 23:26

Asked Pilate for Jesus' body.
Luke 23:50-52

One of the first to hear that Jesus had risen.
Luke 24:1-10

Fill in the numbers; then do the sums!

How many disciples were at Jesus arrest?

Matthew 26:47

How many times Peter did say he didn't know Jesus?

Matthew 26:75

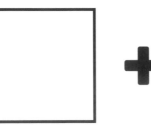 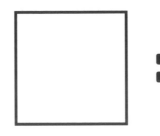 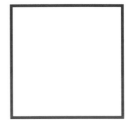

How many silver coins did Judas have?

Matthew 27:3

How many others were crucified with Jesus?

Matthew 27:38

 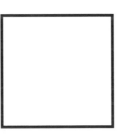 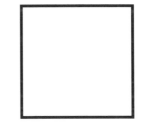

For how many hours did darkness cover the country?

Matthew 27:45-46

How many women watched the burial of Jesus?

Matthew 27:61

  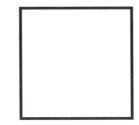

Easter crossword

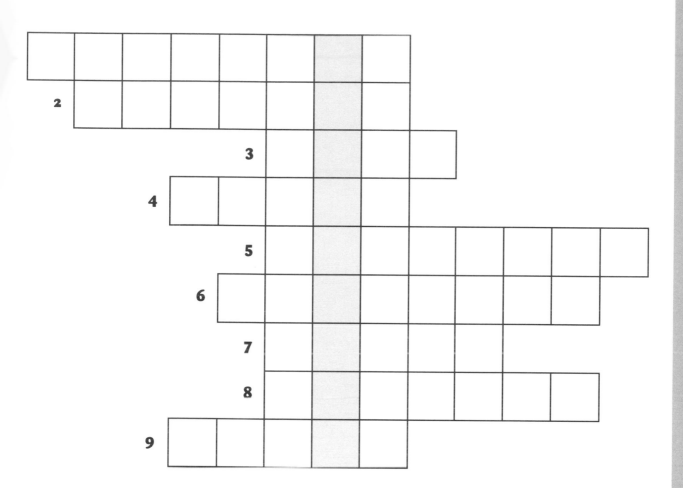

Clues

1 'Place of a Skull'.
Matthew 27:33

2 Divided by those who crucified Jesus.
Matthew 27:35

3 'Jesus, the _ _ _ _ of the Jews.'
Matthew 27:37

4 Jesus was nailed to this.
Matthew 27:31

5 It covered the country for three hours.
Matthew 27:45

6 Men who watched Jesus die.
Matthew 27:54

7 The type of cloth wrapped around Jesus' body.
Matthew 27:59

8 The time of day when Jesus' body was buried.
Matthew 27:57

9 A messenger with very good news!
Matthew 28:5

What was the good news? Read down the shaded column.

Daytime, night-time

A rhyme suitable for summarising part of the story of Easter week

Look, it's daytime, noise and cheering,
Donkey clip-clops, people sing.
Jesus riding, crowds are waving,
Shouting, 'Jesus is our king!'

Now it's night-time, Jesus saying,
'Friends, I'm leaving. It's God's time.'
Friends are weeping, but to help them,
Jesus gives them bread and wine.

It's Passover

A rhyme putting the Last Supper into context

It's Passover, it's Passover,
And Jesus tells his friends,
He's going to die and go away,
This good time's going to end.

It's Passover, it's Passover,
His friends are feeling sad,
But Jesus says he'll come alive
Again – then they'll be glad.

It's Passover, it's Passover,
See Jesus break the bread,
'This is my body, given for you,
Remember me,' he said.

It's Passover, it's Passover,
See Jesus take the wine,
'Remember, when you drink this,
That you are friends of mine.'

And so today, and so today,
We think how Jesus died,
And how he came alive again,
And how his friends all cried.

We won't forget, we won't forget,
What Jesus said that day,
We'll eat the bread and drink the wine,
Remembering him this way.

Here comes our King!

A rhyme for Palm Sunday (which could be sung to the traditional tune 'It's raining, it's pouring')

We're clapping, we're cheering,
Jesus is appearing.
Hosannas ring, here comes our king,
A-riding on a donkey.

We're waving, we're prancing,
Children are all dancing.
Hosannas ring, here comes our king
A-riding on a donkey.

First journey

A rhyme for Palm Sunday

Little donkey standing there
With your grey and shaggy hair,
In the heat and dusty air,
Haven't heard of Jesus.

Tied up to a wooden door,
No one sat on you before.
Saddle, reins, you never wore,
But you're there for Jesus.

Hear the sound of running feet –
Two men come along the street.
They the little donkey greet:
'We need you for Jesus.'

Taken off along the way,
Little donkey does not bray
Though this is the strangest day.
Soon you will meet Jesus.

Ridden by the gentlest man,
Little donkey finds he can
Be a part of God's big plan
And a help to Jesus.

With your king you walk on by,
See the branches waving high,
Hear the noise that fills the sky:
'Shout hooray for Jesus!'

Jesus is alive!

A rhyme with actions which tells the Easter story

Here is the tomb where Jesus lay. *(Line up two fists.)*
Here is the stone that rolled right away. *(Roll away one fist.)*
A bright shining angel *(Wiggle fingers in an arc.)*
Said, 'Come, look inside. *(Beckon with one finger.)*
'Your friend isn't dead. *(Wag one finger back and forth.)*
'Jesus is alive!' *(Throw hands up in joy.)*

Songs and rhymes for younger children

Here is Lord Jesus, *(Put out one hand.)*
And here are his friends. *(Put out other hand.)*
They hug Jesus' feet, *(Clasp wrist with other hand.)*
And shout out again,
Jesus is alive! *(Throw hands up in joy.)*

What do you see?

A rhyme for Easter Day

Say the rhyme, encouraging everyone to join in with the first line of each verse. You could add a rhythm of clapping hands and patting thighs.

Mary, Mary what do you see?
I see an empty grave.
Where can Jesus be?

Peter, Peter, what do you see?
I see the grave clothes.
Where can Jesus be?

Mary, Mary, what do you see?
I see two angels.
Where can Jesus be?

Mary, Mary, what do you see?
I see a gardener.
Where can Jesus be?

Mary, Mary what do you see?
I see Jesus!
He is here with me!

Look and touch

A rhyme, with actions, based on Luke 24:36-53

Puzzled men and women *(Look puzzled.)*
Together in one place. *(Huddle together.)*
Could Jesus really be alive? *(Scratch heads.)*
Would they see his face?

Suddenly he stood there –
Jesus who had died.
All were very frightened. *(Look frightened.)*
'It's just a ghost,' they cried. *(Shiver.)*

'Don't be frightened,' Jesus said.
'It is really me. *(Hold out hands and feet.)*
'See the marks where soldiers
'Nailed me to the tree.' *(Point to palms.)*

'Come and touch me everyone;
'Feel the nail marks too. *(Feel hands, arms etc.)*
'Yes, I really am alive;
'You can see it's true.' *(Point to eyes.)*

Everyone was so amazed,
But still were not quite sure. *(Look doubtful.)*
So Jesus asked, 'Have you some food? *(Rub stomachs.)*
'I need to prove some more.'

They brought a piece of fish for him,
Which Jesus ate to show *(Eat.)*
That he was now alive and well,
As promised long ago.

Later Jesus left them *(Raise palms.)*
And disappeared from view, *(Cover eyes.)*
But first he reassured them,
'I'll always be with you.' *(Cross hands over chest.)*

Easter joy

A rhyme exploring reactions to the resurrection

It was still dark when Mary went out.
She looked around. There was no one about.

She was feeling sad, for Jesus had died,
Nailed to a cross because people had lied.

She went to the cave where Jesus was laid,
But it was empty, the stone rolled away.

Friends Peter and John ran to the tomb;
They saw the cloths lying there in the gloom.

They ran back home. Poor Mary, she cried.
She looked in the cave and two angels she spied.

She turned to a man who was standing nearby.
'Have you taken Jesus?' she asked with a sigh.

Then the man spoke her name and all became clear.
Mary knew it was Jesus. She had nothing to fear.

Now I know

A song reflecting on the events of Jesus' life by Nick Harding

Jesus was born as a baby.
Jesus lived as a man.
Jesus spoke great words of wisdom,
Making clear God's plan.

Chorus:
Now I know, now I see –
Jesus died and lives for me.

Jesus was killed as a robber.
Jesus died in pain.
Jesus knew he had to suffer
And to rise again.

Jesus took all my hurting.
Jesus took all my sin.
Jesus lives to be my friend, so
Real life can begin.

Now I know

Words and music by
Nick Harding

Songs, rhymes and raps

Songs for adults or all ages

My place

An Easter reading for one or more voices by David Shailer

Jesus died for me.

Jesus died in my place.

He did not deserve to die.

He did not deserve to be beaten by soldiers.

He did not deserve to be whipped with leather and barbs that tore his flesh.

He did not deserve a crown of thorns gouged onto his forehead.

He suffered.

His blood flowed freely.

They stretched out his body, taut as a wire, and plunged nails into his wrists and ankles to hold him there.

Then they hoisted him into the sky to be scorched by the sun.

Every breath painful.

And onto him was cast blackness and despair.

Every evil thing that has been or will ever be.

Every torture man has inflicted. Every abuse of body, mind or spirit. Every murder. Every lustful thought. Every angry word. Every selfish act. Every vengeful dream.

The whole ugly black mass of humanity and me a part of it.

He hung there. Taking it all.

Upon himself.

Now *he* was responsible. Now *he* was to blame.

And because he was responsible, he paid the price.

He died for us.

He died for me.

He died in my place.

The Easter rap

A rap with a refrain for more than one voice by Sarah Smart

Yo! Listen up dudes I got some headline news,
It's mind blowin' stuff, so hold on to your pews!
I wanna tell you about da real Easter story.
It ain't about bunnies – in fact it's kinda gory.
See it's all about Jesus, who was flogged 'n' crucified,
Though he'd done no wrong – in fact he'd lived a perfect life.

(Refrain)
One Man (JC)
One Cross (A Tree)
One Price (His blood)
He Paid for us

So check out headline 1: God came down to earth,
He was born as a baby, through the miracle birth.
And tho' he made the world, was heaven's might hero,
He made himself nothin' – a big fat zero.
When his death was near, he rode a donkey into town.
The people called him 'king' and threw the coats down on da ground!

(Refrain)

Now headline 2 is this: Jesus was betrayed,
But he knew that it would happen and he didn't run away.
The night he was arrested, his mates came for a meal,
He told them he was gonna die, and *that* was the deal.
He took some bread and wine and he gave it to his friends,
Sayin' 'Take my blood and body, they give heaven without end.'

(Refrain)

Now headline 3: Jesus died on a cross.
His friends ran away and the soldiers cast lots
For his clothes, while he hung by his feet and his wrists.
He could've come down, but he chose to persist.
For the only time ever, God was parted from his Son –
Jesus took the penalty for the wrongs we have done.

(Refrain)

So headline 4: Why was death Jesus' ambition?
Cos he loved you so much, and forgiveness was
his mission.
It ain't no slushy love like Hollywood portrays,
It was love that wore a crown of thorns 'n' went
to the grave.
As Jesus died, the temple curtain ripped in two
Showing heaven was open to me and to you.

(Refrain)

Check out headline 5: Jesus came back from the
dead.
Mary went to see the body – found an angel
there instead!
He said, 'Yo now Missy Mary, Jesus ain't in the
tomb,
He's conquered sin and death – so forget your
tears and groove!'
The disciples binned their fears, trusted in the
risen Christ.
They proclaimed him to the world – many paid
with their lives.

(Refrain)

Listen up for headline 6: Jesus is alive today.
The angels sing in heaven, 'Jesus rocks and Jesus
saves.'
Though people looked in vain, no body has been
found.
The reason why is pretty clear – he ain't in the
ground!
His mission was accomplished, death's bitten the
dust.
JC's living and true, the one you can trust.

(Refrain)

Resurrection Rap

A rap for two voices

Voice 1
Ain't talking 'bout a corpse,
Ain't talking 'bout a stiff,
I'm talking 'bout my Jesus who's alive.

Voice 2
As if!
Your Jesus is a bloke out of history,
So old he is practically BC!

Voice 1
OK! He's historic but he ain't no fossil,

Just look at what is claimed by Luke the apostle:
Jesus lived and loved and was crucified.
They nailed him to a cross and then he died.

Voice 2
There, see? He's dead! Put that in your pipe and
suck it!
You can't come back when you've kicked the
bucket!

Voice 1
Jesus died, they put his body in a grave,
But three days on, the tomb was empty – what a
rave!
When the women went to look, they saw angels
who said,
'No Jesus ain't here – he's risen from the dead!'
Loads of people saw him, but what convinced
them most,
Was he still could eat his fish and chips – this
guy was no ghost!

Voice 2
But two thousand years ago and many miles
away!
I want a Jesus who is here and now today.

Voice 1
He is! He's alive! A life without end!
He's here and now for all of us and wants to be
our friend!
So put your hands together, let's hear you say:
Jesus Christ is alive today!

The last journey

*A poem that travels from Palm Sunday to Easter
Day and beyond by Marjory Francis*

Travel with Jesus – 'Hosanna!' they cry
Along the palm-strewn road,
As patiently the donkey plods
And bears his precious load.

Travel with Jesus – into the inn
And up the well-worn stairs.
He gives himself – for them, for me –
As bread and wine he shares.
Travel with Jesus – into the night.
The blackness, the darkness outpoured.
But battle is fought, the enemy faced
And victory assured.

Travel with Jesus – dressed in a robe
And mockingly crowned as a king,
Beaten and ridiculed, slandered, ill-tried,
My punishment, his suffering.

Songs for adults or all ages

Travel with Jesus – bearing a cross,
The hillside of horror ahead,
The nails, the pain, the load of sin –
He took them in my stead.

No need to travel – it is done,
His life at an end.
The garden cave a resting place
For this my dearest friend.

But travel with Jesus – into Life!
Mary, Peter – see!
He rises from death that Sunday morn
Unlimited and free,
And living still, he grasps my hand
And travels now with me.

Easter morning

A poem based on John 20:1-18 by Marjory Francis

In the darkness before morning,
In the cool before the day,
Ere the sunrise and the dawning
Chase the shadows and the grey,
Comes a whisper soft and clear,
'He is not here.'

As the first soft rays of young light
Long and strange the shadows trace,
Dewdrops glisten in the sunlight,
Mirrored on a weeping face.
'Fear not, wipe away your tear.
'He is not here.'

Small tight buds begin uncurling
Vivid petals, fresh and rare.
Perfume trapped, but with unfurling,
Now released to scent the air,
Announcing words of joy, not fear,
'He is not here.'

Birds sing melodies of wonder
Giving praise to God alone.
Earth joins in with drumming thunder –
Quaking ground and shifting stone.
All of nature makes it clear:
'He is not here.'

Not for us the angels shining
'Mongst the scents and songbirds' praise,
Spoken message underlining
What the empty tomb conveys.
Today, for us, his presence near
Says, 'I am here.'

In obedience

A poem based on Matthew 11:28-30 by Marjory Francis

In obedience
To earth he came,
Becoming a man
He took the yoke of this world's pain.

Jesus, vulnerable child,
In a manger born –
A king, but destined to be crowned with thorn.

In obedience
He took the cross,
And on himself
Was poured out all my sin and dross.

Jesus, setting fast his face
To Calvary,
Carrying my burden, sets me free.

In obedience
He breathed his last,
And all my sins
Were paid for, vanished in the past.

Jesus, buried in the cave
For three short days;
My sins he left there, as to life he's raised.

In obedience
To him I give
My heart and soul.
I take his burden light – and live.

Jesus, my glorious Lord,
Your yoke on me
Is all I need, and be set free.

He is the one

A poem about Jesus' identity from birth to resurrection by Marjory Francis.

He is the one who, at his birth
Slept in a humble bed of hay.
He is the one who walked the earth
Helping others day by day.
He is the one.

He is the one who for followers close
The workman, the rebel, the outcast, the thief.
He is the one who welcomed all those
Who were sick or rejected or stricken with grief.
He is the one.

He is the one with power to control
The sea to a clam from an angry mood.
He is the one who made people whole
And fed them with his eternal food.
He is the one.

He is the one who heard the crowd
Change from loud praises to cries for blood.
He is the one whose head was bowed
As his hands were nailed to a cross of wood.
He is the one.

He is the one, with the clouds above
Darkening the sun in the noonday sky,
Spread his arms in an act of love.
He is the one who chose to die.
He is the one.

He is the one who, after the night,
Victory secured, for the battle is won,
Rising from death in glorious light,
Showed to his followers that he is the One
Saviour and Lord, yes, you are The One!

Crosswords

A cross-shaped poem by Marjory Francis.

A real tree has died
and from it made
a makeshift tree,
where hangs a man
to all the world displayed.
Who is this man, whose arms spread wide,
expose his heart of love for all on earth?
Whose hands uncurled in giving, are denied,
instead are pierced to show our worth;
and as the blood is flowing from his side,
his agonising death brings me new birth,
and life
and peace
and freedom
in my soul,
and hope
and faith
to make
me whole;
ten, twenty
thousand
benefits,
and more
beside,
and always
his companionship,
my everlasting guide.

All poems by Marjory Francis
© Marjory Francis

Songs, rhymes and raps

92

Quotes and anecdotes for Easter

Celebration

In August 2001 the streets of Liverpool were packed with people from all over the world celebrating a Beatles Festival. It is nearly forty years since the 'Fab Four' rocked the world with their music, yet they are still fondly remembered by many. In the same way, Jerusalem was filled with people from many parts of the world to celebrate their deliverance by God, and Jesus wished to be part of that too.

Openness

A Christian counsellor was being interviewed about his work and some of the difficulties he faced as a Christian. When asked about his response to those who approach him with a different set of moral values, he replied: 'We have to learn to accept all sorts of people without necessarily approving of their behaviour.' This was Jesus' attitude to his two disloyal disciples.

The Lord's Supper

'The Last Supper was Jesus in dramatic prophetic action saying, "Look, this is what they are going to do to me – but what is going to happen to me is for you." In this Jesus was walking in the tradition of the prophets, and using this dramatic action to make men see what stated in words they refused to see and understand.'
(William Barclay, *The Lord's Supper*, SCM, 1967.)

Opinions about resurrection

'Christian Research has come up with some cheering news for Easter. When it asked people whether they believed that Christ rose from the dead, 47 per cent said that they did. Praise be! 36 per cent said they didn't. But what of the 15 per cent of the population who mumbled 'Don't know'? Don't know? Sir, madam, the question was not one of fact – whether Lima is the capital of Peru – it was one of instinct, of what you feel in the depths of your soul. Of course none of us knows that Jesus rolled back that boulder and revealed himself. If we did, it would no longer be the great Christian mystery, would it? The question was whether in your own heart you have faith in the truth of that unknown. What the dithering 15 per cent are saying is that they don't know what they think about not knowing.'
('Thunderer' column in *The Times*, 19 April 2003.)

True story

I was walking down our main shopping street the other day when a car coming up the street caught my eye. The multi-pierced, sun-glassed youth driving it was leaning out of the window, shouting at any attractive girls he saw. His car sounded as if it was powered solely by music. Whilst life isn't always as delicious as this I was gratified when, through lack of attention, he drove into the back of the car in front. Except that I can't say this happened for sure. I saw him as he passed me and I heard the crash and then turned round. I didn't see the accident. The car in front may have reversed into him for all I know, unlikely as this seems. A lawyer would make mincemeat of me. You can only witness what you have seen.
(Steve Tilley)

Punchlines

Read out some punch lines to a few well-known jokes. See if anyone can 'guess the joke'. Jokes make no sense without the punch lines, and they belong at the end. The punch line to Jesus' life and death is his resurrection. His teaching makes no sense without it. It is useless.

SEP

In one of the *Hitchhiker's Guide to the Galaxy* series of books, the late Douglas Adams wrote of a huge spaceship powered by an SEP drive. This stood for 'Somebody Else's Problem'. If people didn't believe the spaceship was anything to do with them, they simply failed to 'see' it. John tells us that deciding what to think about Jesus is everybody's problem and his story is written to help us see him properly (John 20:31).

Amnesty

Peter Benenson died at the beginning of 2005. In his long life, he must have done and said many significant things. But imagine telling his life story without mentioning Amnesty International, which he founded. Thousands of people worldwide owe their lives and freedom to the campaigning organisation which was his initiative. Imagine telling the story of Jesus' life without mentioning his death and resurrection. Millions of people owe their life and freedom to his sacrificial love.
(Christine Wright)

For Christmas

Christmas Wrapped Up!

£8.99
1 85999 795 3

New material and favourites from SALT

Christmas Wrapped up!

Parties Plays
Crafts Events
Service outlines
and everything your church
might need at Christmas
(well almost everything!)

Scripture union

At last – the ultimate Christmas resource book! It really does contain practically everything a church might need for Christmas time. Includes service outlines, yuletide evangelism, plays, quiz questions, songs, craft, parties and games.

New material and Scripture Union favourites

Celebrations sorted

Great resources for:

Remembrance Sunday

Mothering Sunday

Pentecost

New Year

Valentine's Day

Harvest

and much, much more!

Celebrations Sorted

£8.99

1 84427 182 X

Celebrations Sorted is packed full of ideas for you to use at times of celebration in the church calendar. Includes service outlines, craft, drama, assemblies, creative prayer and much, much more.